No God or Only God

No God or Only God

W. H. S. Gebel

Suluk Press

Richmond, Virginia

Published by Sulūk Press

112 East Cary Street | Richmond, Virginia 23219
sulukpress.com

Copy editor: Rebecca Sadlon
Editor: Cannon Labrie
Cover design: Missy Reynolds of Clothilde Designs

Printed on acid-free paper.

Image credits:
Page 22, from https://en.wikiversity.org/wiki/File:Limbic_System.png; created by SoniaM2020, October 20, 2020. Licensed under Creative Commons Attribution-Share Alike 4.0 International.
Page 24, image created by OpenStax College, Anatomy & Physiology, Connexions website, https://openstax.org/books/anatomy-and-physiology/pages/1-introduction.
Page 28, image of the brain's limbic system reproduced with permission of the creator Todd Murhpy in his book *Sacred Pathways: The Brain's Role in Sacred and Mystic Experiences*.
Page 96, Feynman diagram from *QED: The Strange Theory of Light and Matter* (Princeton, NJ: Princeton University Press, 2006), reproduced with permission of Princeton University Press.
Page 100, Process of Translation from yourgenome.org reproduced with permission of the creator Laura Olivares Boldú at Wellcome Connecting Science.
Page 148 images from DrBob at the English-language Wikipedia, https://en.wikipedia.org/wiki/Holography. Licensed under Creative Commons Attribution-Share Alike 3.0 Unported license.

ISBN 978-1-941810-47-7 (paper)
ISBN 978-1-941810-48-4 (e-book)

Names: Gebel, W. H. S., 1941–, author. |
Title: No God or Only God
Description: First Edition. Richmond, VA: Sulūk Press, 2024. | Includes preface.
Identifiers: LCCN 2024939285 | ISBN 9781941810477 (paper) |
ISBN 9781941810484 (e-book)
Subjects: LCSH: Sufism | BISAC: Religion/Sufi | Religion/Mysticism

Printed and bound in the United States of America

Contents

Part 4: A Stepping-Stone

Preface

WHEN I WROTE *Nature's Hidden Dimension: Envisioning the Inner Life of the Universe* (Sulūk Press, 2018), I deliberately avoided using the word "God," speaking instead of pure intelligence. I did so because "God" has a variety of meanings for different readers and often is controversial. I wanted to remove a potential barrier that might prevent readers from impartially considering the ideas I presented.

There is a large body of literature advocating atheism that goes back to Lucretius and includes prominent thinkers such as Baruch Spinoza, Percy Bysshe Shelley, Charles Darwin, Mark Twain, Sigmund Freud, Albert Einstein, and Carl Sagan.[1] Contemporary thinkers like Richard Dawkins, Daniel Dennett, and Christopher Hitchens have written popular books calling for the philosophy of humanism to replace religion and claiming that belief in a personal God is an anachronism.

Some religious thinkers have taken offense at the aggressive stance taken by the scientist Richard Dawkins in his well-known book, *The God Delusion*. Many have written books answering his challenges and defending their faith, and some have met with him in public debate. As a fellow scientist, I sympathize with the sincerity of Dawkins's examination of belief in God. I appreciate his vision of humanism as a

1. See Christopher Hitchens, ed., *The Portable Atheist: Essential Readings for the Nonbeliever* (Philadelphia: Da Capo Press, 2007).

source of meaning in life and as a repository of human wisdom providing an ethical basis for living rightly.

Science has demonstrated its superiority in revealing the workings of the outer life of the universe. In a famous anecdote, Napoleon questioned the renowned physicist Pierre Laplace about his recently completed treatise on celestial mechanics. He asked Laplace how he could write an account of the universe, leaving out the Creator? Laplace replied, "I had no need for that hypothesis." Yet, there is a realm of knowledge science cannot reach: the inner life of the universe. There is nothing there that can be measured.

Scientists study the material world. Mystics explore the world of mind and spirit. In daily life, we experience the world from the perspective of dualism: subject and object. Our description and grasp of things depends on comparisons. This is like that. When we look more deeply, we see everywhere an ecology. Apparently independent entities depend on a system of relationships.

The Buddha recognized that nothing has an independent existence. Thich Nhat Hanh said simply, "This is because that is. This is not, because that is not."[2] As we examine the ecology of the universe, we see things aggregating in wholes, and how larger wholes depend on collections of smaller wholes. If we examine our life and notion of self, we begin to see that we are not the separate, isolated individuals we may have thought we were. We are shaped and molded by all sorts of influences constantly at work.

Mystics experience the profound awakening of unity. They lose their sense of boundedness and merge with all beings and things. Radically different from dualism, philosophers have called this a nondual perception of reality. That

---

2. *Old Path, White Clouds: The Life Story of Buddha* (Berkeley, CA: Parallax Press, 1991), 605.

nondual state is a state of being. That being is the One Being. Is this what is meant by God?

The awakening experienced by mystics is called Self-realization. If it were described as self-realization, it would be an achievement of the ordinary self, a victory of the ego. But then it would still be dualistic and complicated by claims and comparisons. If it is Self-realization, it is a realization of the one universal Self. It is not my Self—I don't own it—but the Self that is present in every thing and every being. Trying to achieve Self-realization by one's own efforts is like trying to pull oneself up by one's bootstraps.

This book describes a method of seeking Self-realization passed down by mystics in the Sufi tradition. One takes responsibility to create one's own God ideal. This is a conception of God that comes from within. It comes from one's inherent values and ideals. By making this ideal alive, one awakens something that has been dormant in one's inner life. Through the power of love and imagination, one brings to life in oneself what was waiting and wanting to emerge.

Recognizing this method as a legitimate way to reach Self-realization, one can honor whatever conception of God one discovers in oneself and any conception of God one finds in others. There is no right way to conceive of God. There is no correct belief in God. Every belief is a step on the way to fulfilling the kind of promise one sees in each newborn child.

My own adventure in coming to know my God ideal has helped me keep an open mind and heart when encountering the beliefs of others. We are all on the same journey, each with our own mission and unique gifts. Our belief in our own God ideal holds a key for unlocking the door to the hidden treasure that is our common heritage.

Part 1

No God

1

Atheism

The world would be astonished if it knew how great a propor-
tion of its brightest ornaments—of those most distinguished
even in popular estimation for wisdom and virtue—are complete skeptics in religion; many of them refraining from avowal,
less from personal considerations, than from a conscientious-
ness, though now in my opinion a most mistaken apprehension
lest by speaking out what would tend to weaken existing beliefs,
and by consequence (as they suppose) existing restraints, they
should do harm instead of good.
—John Stuart Mill, *Autobiography*

During the youthful period of mankind's spiritual evolution
human fantasy created gods in man's own image, who, by the
operations of their will were supposed to determine, or at any
rate to influence, the phenomenal world. Man sought to alter
the disposition of these gods in his own favor by means of magic
and prayer. The idea of God in the religions taught at present is
a sublimation of that old concept of the gods. Its anthropomorphic character is shown for instance, by the fact that men appeal
to the Divine Being in prayers and plead for the fulfillment of
their wishes.
—Albert Einstein, "Science, Philosophy, and Religion,"
in *Out of My Later Years*

AN EXPLORATION OF the word "God" needs to start with
an acknowledgment of the eloquent words and arguments
of those who promote atheism. Atheism has a long and
distinguished history in the West, largely stemming from the
time of the Enlightenment in the seventeenth and eighteenth

centuries. The spectacular success of science in explaining the mysteries of the natural world, developing modern medicine, improving the economic welfare of the world, and producing the modern miracles of technology has challenged the authority of religion step-by-step. And now a sincere and outspoken movement has declared that religion is no longer needed, that what they call the God hypothesis can be investigated scientifically, that belief in a personal God is a stubborn superstition we have outgrown but are reluctant to acknowledge, and that there are aspects of religion that are harmful and dangerous that need to be recognized and addressed.

Polls have consistently shown that professed atheism is not common in the Western world. According to a 2010 Pew Research global study, the percentage of atheists in Europe was 12 percent, in North America 5 percent, in Latin America 4 percent, in the Middle East and North Africa 2 percent, and in the south of Africa 1 percent. By contrast in Asia, particularly China, the percentage was 76 percent. However, because traditional religions in China are nontheistic, this percentage does not necessarily reflect religious belief. In academia in the West the percentage of atheists is much higher than in the average population. For example, a poll in 2014 among academic philosophers had 73 percent describing themselves as atheists.[1] These results appear to indicate that the more one is educated, the greater the likelihood one might reject the idea of a personal God.

Let's consider the point of view of a modern atheist. A popular book that lays out the case for rejecting belief in a personal God is Richard Dawkins's *The God Delusion.* Dawkins examines the question of whether God exists from many perspectives. Among the many themes he discusses, he con-

1. David Bourget and David J. Chalmers, "What Do Philosophers Believe?" *Philosophical Studies* 170, no. 3 (2014): 465–500.

siders the origins of religion, the God hypothesis, traditional proofs of the existence of God, harm caused by religion, and an alternative humanistic worldview.

The Origins of Religion

One might reasonably imagine that religion began as a superstitious belief that it is the influence of gods that controls nature's sometimes frightening mysteries. There are many examples of early cultures worldwide that have explained threatening or awe-inspiring natural phenomena through an oral tradition of stories about deities or supernatural beings.

The rising and setting of the sun, the changing of the seasons, the phases of the moon, shooting stars and comets, eclipses, earthquakes, storms and lightning, floods and famine, and many other natural phenomena must have been objects of wonder or fear for early humans. As these events stunned imagination, it was natural for early humans to assume that they had a supernatural and sacred origin. Children often feel they must be to blame for misfortunes in their lives, and in a similar way primitive peoples might have felt that their actions or thoughts were responsible for fearful events. They could hope that supplications, ritual offerings, and observance of taboos would appease supernatural agents that were expressing displeasure with human actions.

Today, we don't take these stories of deities seriously. It is easy for many of us to reject deities that were sacred to earlier peoples. A modern atheist would say we have given up many deities. We have only one small step to take to give up the one that remains.

According to this perspective, one could view religion today as a holdover from this primitive grasping after security in the face of the uncertainties of life. Much of humanity has believed for so long that our destiny is in the hands of a supernatural agency. Do we believe consciously or unconsciously that without having a relationship of penance and reassurance with that controller of events, we will be at the mercy of cold and uncaring forces of nature? Freud viewed religious feeling as wish fulfillment or the perpetuation of an illusion. Hawkins calls it the God Delusion.

An atheist would say that religious belief has come from superstition and wishful thinking. And now through the rational and empirical tools of science, humanity has reached the point where mysterious and threatening phenomena are understandable without invoking supernatural displeasure. That primitive need for explanation and the appeasement of powerful beings is obsolete. Science has shown not only that mysteries have natural explanations but also that we can turn our knowledge of phenomena to practical use through technology. In the atheist's view, we no longer need to invoke a supernatural controller; now we are ready to take responsibility ourselves for responding to natural phenomena and controlling events. This is the human challenge of our age. It is time to put away our childish fears and take full responsibility for our actions. We can no longer look for a savior to rescue us from our follies.

If superstition is supposed to be the origin of religious belief, what about the further development of religion through revelation—for example, the Western religions of Judaism, Christianity, and Islam? The great prophets such as Moses, Jesus, and Muhammad (peace be upon them) each felt instructed to serve and raise the consciousness of humanity to a higher level of compassion and generosity. Their version of religion was not primarily a teaching to explain how nature works. Although the stories of their revelations include miracles and homage to God as Creator and Sustainer, they didn't offer supernatural explanations for natural events as in earlier religions. What they chiefly offered was a way to live with dignity, honor, and consideration for others. Dawkins applauds the kindness and self-sacrifice, for example, of Jesus. However, representing the rationality of atheists, he doesn't accept the miracle stories, the efficacy of prayer, or the judging or protective role of a deity.

One who believes in the explanatory power of science and the universality of the laws of nature is naturally skeptical of miracle stories. Can there be exceptions to natural law? The philosopher Spinoza believed that miracles are natural events whose explanations have not yet been discovered. Canonization in the Catholic faith requires proof in most cases of two miracles. Most that are approved by the Church are miracles of healing. To gain the endorsement of the Church as "worthy to be believed in," healing miracles must be thoroughly examined with modern medical tests and not admit of any known medical explanation. A skeptic would ask, "Why does one person receive the special attention of a supernatural intervention when so many other deserving persons are passed over? Why would God wait for the prayers of a saintly person before acting when God being omniscient knows the needs and worthiness of all who are suffering?"

Miracle stories about the prophets such as Moses, Jesus, and Muhammad may be apocryphal legends passed along by well-meaning followers. Such sensational stories would appeal to nonbelievers who might be inclined to scoff at claims of prophethood. With this proof of supernatural power, they would be ready to benefit from the moral and spiritual teachings offered from revelation.

If religions of our day originate from the revelations of prophets who were seeking relief for the suffering of humanity, does the reasoning that humans have outgrown the insecurity of ignorance about natural phenomena apply to today's ideas about God? Have we in the West outgrown the wisdom imparted by the Abrahamic religions? A thoroughgoing atheist might counter with "What wisdom?" Dawkins examines the wisdom of the Scriptures—the Bible and Qur'an—and finds them not only lacking in moral value but even setting a terrible example. He cites many biblical stories that suggest horrendous and immoral behaviors as either commanded by or overlooked by God. Should such stories be defended by those who believe in the divine origins of the scriptures? The rationalist view, even for many liberal Christians, is that the Bible is a collection of narratives that includes inspired revelations along with an oral history that privileges a particular culture and its cultural mores. Many things that were considered acceptable and normal in ancient times are now rejected as unjust, inhumane, or worse. Slavery and the mistreatment of women are two glaring examples.

Furthermore, the impression of God in the Old Testament seen through the eyes of a rational atheist conveys the worst characteristics of a domineering, bloodthirsty bully. Are we as humans meant to cower, look down meekly, ashamed of our shortcomings, and not speak up about the poor role model we are supposed to emulate? In the New Testament, the image of God is better—a kind and loving father figure, aware of every hair on our head, ready to give us all we need. But then, what of the burden of sin we are supposed to carry, and the threat of endless hell if we make a misstep in life? Where did this come from? Are we inspired to live a life of love and generosity, or do we feel threatened with punishment if we do not follow the rules?

Dawkins argues that we don't need scriptures to lead a moral life. The Golden Rule, "Do unto others as you would have them do unto you," is embedded in our culture. The mores of contemporary society have imbibed the wisdom of the Abrahamic religions that are now incorporated into a secular way of life called humanism. As rational thinkers, we no longer need preachers to tell us how to behave or the threat of divine punishment if we transgress. Biblical stories are now archaic, perhaps to be replaced by the sharing of inspiring stories from our own time.

Humanism and existentialism both put their faith in the human being. Freed by science from the superstitious belief in deities and saviors, we are challenged to rise to the occasion and with courage create meaning in our lives. Faced with a universe that operates mechanically, not caring about our welfare or existence, it is up to us to make our lives worthwhile and to adhere to our moral instincts of caring for each other and aspiring to excellence. This is what the outspoken atheists of today passionately affirm. Sweep away the superstitions of the past that we cling to and look with optimism toward a future based on honest inquiry into the awesome mysteries of nature. We can appreciate the beauty and elegance of what is all around us, value our ability to uncover nature's secrets and improve our lives, and seek a life of mutual understanding and compassion.

The God Hypothesis

Originally proposed by Carl Sagan, the God hypothesis claims that the question of the existence of God can be explored by science because it has implications science can investigate. Dawkins qualifies the God hypothesis specifically to apply to a supernatural intelligence that designed and created the universe. He is also speaking of a personal God with whom one can have a relationship of prayer, being judged and forgiven, and being loved and nurtured. As a specialist in neo-Darwinism, he advocates that the appearance of creative intelligence capable of design and production can only come about through a long process of evolution from simple beginnings.

For Dawkins, the decisive event that convinced him to become an atheist was his discovery of Darwin's theory of evolution. Like many biologists and naturalists who marvel at the intricacy and complexity of living systems, Dawkins first saw that the apparent evidence strongly suggested an intelligent designer at work. The brilliance of Darwin's discovery is that a simple mechanism, working slowly over eons of time, guided by the principle of incremental improvements in fitness, could lead to the appearance of intelligent design. By demonstrating that the fossil record shows the gradual development of species from simple to more complex organisms, paleontologists confirmed Darwin's ideas.

Once Darwin was able to show that the need for a hidden designer with superhuman intelligence was unnecessary, the strongest argument for the existence of God was undermined. Although many have labored to come up with a theory of intelligent design to counter Darwin's discovery, so far none have been able to convince skeptical scientists.

What about the other part of the God hypothesis: a personal God in relationship with each worshipper? Although this can't be examined by science, what about its implications? When our planet seemed to be at the center of the universe and the heavens were envisioned as crystalline spheres circling the earth, it was easier to imagine that life on earth was the only life that existed. It made sense that the Creator of our unique environment was intimately interested in its creatures and personal communication was conceivable.

Today, our picture of the cosmos has changed radically. How insignificant we are in space and time. In space, our planet circles an ordinary star located about halfway across the galactic disk from the center. There are approximately one hundred billion stars in our galaxy and more than one hundred billion galaxies like ours spread throughout the universe. Why would the Creator of all of this take an interest in such a tiny and ordinary spot in the cosmos? Of the eight billion souls on our planet, why would God communicate with this one and not that one?

The universe has existed for 13.8 billion years. Human-like creatures have been around for at most three million years, or 0.02 percent of the age of the universe. Has the personal God of relationship only come into existence in the last flicker of a moment? Was there no God of relationship during 99.98 percent of the time the universe has existed when there was no one to have a relationship with?

Proofs of the Existence of God

Theologians like Thomas Aquinas proposed proofs of the existence of God based on logic. These proofs were influenced by the logical and mathematical thinking of the Greek philosophers. Let's consider some of the classical theological proofs of God.

The Unmoved Mover. A change in movement—from stillness or from prior movement—requires a force, or mover. Assuming that each force or mover requires a prior mover, there must have been an original mover that was not moved itself, in other words, the source of all movement. Newton showed that change of movement or acceleration requires a force. An example of a simple force is a push. This is a mechanical movement that results from an expenditure of energy such as muscles contracting.

The source of energy on the earth is the sun. The sun's energy comes from thermonuclear reactions in its core that depend on temperature and pressure brought about by gravity. Gravitational energy can be traced back to the big bang. Electromagnetic forces can also be traced back to the creation of charged particles in the big bang. Though the source of the big bang has not yet been explained by science, cosmologist Stephen Hawking felt confident that eventually it will be. Being able to explain how the big bang came about, generating an expanding universe from nothing (the flickering existence of elementary particles in a vacuum) would offer a scientific explanation of the Prime Mover, the source of all motion and energy.

The Uncaused Cause. In the stream of cause and effect, each effect must be preceded by a cause. If we trace back in time through the chain of cause and effect, we ultimately reach the first cause or the source of causes. Because we are limited to the finite age of the universe, we can't go back indefinitely. Again, we are led back to the big bang and its anticipated explanation from theories of physics. If physics can explain the source of motion and energy, presumably it can also explain the initiating cause that triggered the phenomenon of the universe.

The Cosmological Argument. Matter and energy are conserved. Physical things exist now that have emerged from physical things of the past. Theologians assume there was a time when no physical things existed. They conclude that physical things came from something nonphysical. Theologians who contrived this argument knew nothing about the big bang and the expanding universe. Today, we could imagine that before the big bang there were no physical things. Or, if there were, they were not able to emerge from the twilight existence of the zero-point energy or vacuum state of quantum mechanics. This argument awaits further scientific understanding of the origin of the universe.

Dawkins makes the point that each of these arguments originally assumed there could be something that stops the chain of regression, a source that differs basically from everything else. He asks: Why do we assume there is a stopping point? Can the regression go on indefinitely? In other words, why is God not moved by a prior force, or why does God not have a prior cause, or why is God not some form of matter or energy? On the other hand, if there is a stopping point or unique source, why call it God? Why would it have other characteristics of God such as omnipotence or omniscience?

The Argument by Design. If God is the Creator and Designer of the universe, the simplest challenge is to ask who or what created God. In this respect, this argument is like the previous arguments that require a unique source that is unmoved or uncaused or uncreated. Otherwise, we have the situation of an infinite regress illustrated by the mythology of the world supported on the back of a turtle and that turtle supported on the back of another turtle, and so on; it's turtles all the way down. If the first turtle had no need for support being the unsupported supporter, this would be the case of a unique source basically different from everything else.

We have previously seen how Darwinian evolution gives a simple explanation for how apparently intelligent design in living organisms can arise without the need for an intelligent designer. This is one aspect of the Argument by Design and was enough for Richard Dawkins to feel confident in adopting atheism. He felt that God the intelligent Creator is not needed to explain how marvelously life is designed.

However, there is still an unsolved mystery about how life originated on earth. There are scientific proposals for how this could have happened spontaneously through chemical reactions catalyzed by, for example, clays as stabilizing materials. Plausibility arguments can be made but there is so far no proof of any proposed mechanism.

Then there is the further problem of how inanimate materials were created. Where did the first elementary particles come from? Once again, we have to go back to the first moments of the big bang and ask how matter could emerge from the flickering vacuum. There is also the question of how the unified forces could emerge. And beyond that, how did space and time arise? These are questions about whether a Creator is needed to explain the origin of the universe. For Stephen Hawking, they represent the scientist's confrontation with atheism or belief. If scientists can explain how matter, basic forces, and time and space came about without the need for a Creator, then the Argument by Design will be overcome.

A classic argument against the existence of God is the problem of the existence of evil. If God is omnipotent and benevolent, then how could God stand by when vast numbers of innocents are murdered in genocides? Generations of Jews were alienated from their religion by the tragedy of the Holocaust. The twentieth century saw many other examples of genocides. Natural disasters also take many innocent lives. The tsunami in Asia in 2004 killed more than 225,000 people. Why would a God who has intervened in history to save favored people from disaster stand by when so many worthy souls were wiped out? The logical conclusion would be that either God is not omnipotent and not able to intervene, or God is not benevolent and caring, or wishes harm. An atheist would say the easiest answer is there is no God. Humans are responsible for overcoming the fear and hatred of the other that leads to genocide. Natural disasters will happen. The best we can do is improve our early warning systems and use technology to protect ourselves as best we can when disaster strikes.

Does Religion Cause Harm?

It is commonly assumed that most wars arise from religious conflict. Terrorism by religious extremists in our time seems to confirm this belief. However, scholars have examined this idea objectively and concluded that only a small minority of wars can be attributed to religious differences. More common causes of war include the desire for power and control, ethnic intolerance, economic and political gain, and nationalism.

In their recently published book, *Encyclopedia of Wars*, authors Charles Phillips and Alan Axelrod document the history of recorded warfare. From their list of 1,763 wars, only 123 have been classified to involve a religious cause, accounting for less than 7 percent of all wars and less than 2 percent of all people killed in warfare.[2]

Although the doctrine of the Abrahamic religions promotes peace and forgiveness, the history of each of the religions is filled with examples of conquest and dominance. Dawkins gives examples from the Torah of commands by God to slaughter those of other beliefs, to have no mercy for women and children. Though Jesus entreated, "Love your enemies," Christians justified torturing Jews and Muslims in the Inquisition by claiming it was done to save their souls. And of course, the Crusades were a gruesome fight to regain control of the Holy Lands, which happened to be holy for the other side as well. Muslims have also engaged in holy wars to bring, as they see it, the true religion to the infidels.

In our own time, we have seen extremists of each of the Abrahamic religions justify terrorist or oppressive acts based on their beliefs. We have seen widespread sexual abuse in the Catholic Church. We have seen ethnic cleansing reflecting religious hatreds. We have seen oppression of women in the name of religion. Certainly, we don't have to look far to see harm caused by religious beliefs.

On a cultural level, atheists can point to miseries caused by the imposition of strict moral codes by the more orthodox versions of religion. Not following these codes can lead to physical punishment, arrest, shaming, shunning, or even murder. Such codes can implant in a sincere devotee a punishing superego that taunts the believer with the threat of eternal punishment in hell.

Dawkins makes a special case against the indoctrination of children. Before they are able to reason for themselves,

2. Rabbi Alan Lurie, "Is Religion the Cause of Most Wars?," *Huffington Post*, June 10, 2012.

they are often taught to be faithful to a particular belief. As children, they trust those who have authority over them, their parents, teachers, and religious authorities. Those who are skeptical by nature may escape by rebellion as teenagers. Those who are more docile or accepting may fear to free themselves from the authorities of their childhood. They may judge themselves for doubts that arise rather than feeling welcomed as adults to make up their own minds. Dawkins feels that children should be taught that they have the right to decide what to believe when they mature.

Humanism

The Age of Enlightenment promised a bright future for humanity. No longer were knowledge and therefore power the province of the authority of royalty and church. From classical times, knowledge had been derived from philosophical or theological principles but now the principles were put to the test. Experimentation and demonstration proved to be more reliable pathways to knowledge. Science was discovering universal laws of nature that not only unveiled the workings of nature but also provided the tools of technology to improve human welfare. Industry gradually raised the standard of living for the masses. The spirit of egalitarianism replaced monarchy with democracy. Discoveries in medicine improved the overall health and extended the average lifetime.

The dramatic progress of scientific discovery led to the expectation at the end of the nineteenth century that soon the general laws of nature would be understood and only the details would remain to be uncovered. Nature was predictable, deterministic, and mechanical. From this confidence, scientists felt that all topics of inquiry would eventually yield their secrets to scientific scrutiny.

The fresh spirit of the Enlightenment with its emphasis on empiricism and reason noted how religion, once the ultimate authority for the masses, had to back down step-by-step. First came Copernicus with his simplification of the orbits of planets by making the sun rather than the earth the center of the universe and the earth one among many planets orbiting the sun. Then Kepler demonstrated that planetary orbits are ellipses instead of circles, another blow to ancient principles. Newton showed that planetary orbits obey the universal law of gravitation. They are impelled by the same force that causes apples to fall from trees. There is no need for planets to be attached to crystalline spheres or for a Prime Mover to set them in motion. Then, with the discovery of extinct animals' fossils and the dating of geological formations, religion again had to back down from its story of creation and the implied age of the earth. With the theory of evolution, the story of creation took another blow. God the Creator was no longer needed to explain the apparent design in nature. In more recent times, the developing story of the big bang and the expanding universe has once more challenged religious ideas of the centrality and specialness of the earth and of a Creator at the beginning of time.

As scientific discoveries and theories replaced the need for religious explanations, it was natural for the scientifically minded to question whether any reason remained to worship a God who seemed irrelevant in the scientific worldview. The Enlightenment envisioned a society guided by reason, steadily progressing toward a better life for everyone. With its deeper understanding of the laws of nature, humanity could now take responsibility for controlling its destiny. Humanism adopted the basic moral code espoused by religion, a code of kindness, forgiveness, caring, and mutual responsibility. Humanists believe that adherence to this code does not require religious authority or fearful awareness of a judging God watching over our shoulders. Our feeling about what is right has either evolved toward greater compassion or it is an inherent aspect of our nature that can better emerge when our lives are secure.

Dawkins ends *The God Delusion* with a vision of a world free of the superstitions of the past. Without the assumptions and expectations that have been passed down culturally, humanity can be free to explore the wide universe with an open mind. Scientists are excited to gain an ever-greater understanding of how nature works. They view religious beliefs as a narrow window on the world. Once we free ourselves of this unnecessary limitation, what wonders await us? We are fortunate to be alive at a time when so much is being discovered at a rapid pace. This is something to celebrate.

A Deeply Religious Nonbeliever

Are atheists devoid of the feeling of sacredness? Do they live in a cold dry materialistic reality, in an uncaring mechanistic world? Certainly not. Dawkins and others convey in their writings caring and compassion. They believe they are espousing a healthy and realistic worldview. They feel a duty to warn and to campaign against the abuses and harm that religious beliefs have caused.

There is a form of religion that some atheists have affirmed. Spinoza and Einstein have been cited as holding views exemplifying this form of religion. If there is such a thing as God, it is not a personal God with human characteristics, not a God whom one can worship or to whom one can offer prayers. Rather, God is to be found in the wonder and awe that nature inspires. The scientist encounters this recognition of God in the elegant orderliness of the universe, in the intricate workings and complexity of nature's designs, in the mathematical beauty of the relationships of things.

I have never imputed to Nature a purpose or a goal, or anything that could be understood as anthropomorphic.

What I see in Nature is a magnificent structure that we can comprehend only very imperfectly, and that must fill a thinking person with a feeling of humility. This is a genuinely religious feeling that has nothing to do with mysticism.[3]

Dawkins sees himself as a deeply religious nonbeliever. In the beauty and wonder of nature, he feels there is something inspiring, something sacred. In this the humanist and the religious believer can agree, that life is worthwhile and meaningful, that we are fortunate to be alive, that there is a feeling of magic that life offers, because of a shared feeling of sacredness and wonder.

---

3. Albert Einstein in Helen Dukas and Banesh Hoffman, *Albert Einstein: The Human Side* (Princeton, NJ: Princeton University Press, 1979), 39.

2

Neurotheology

A RATIONAL EXAMINATION of the idea of God and the question of whether God exists leads in the end to atheism. What about other ways one might come to a belief in God? A beautiful work of art moves and inspires us with a sense of meaning, not through rational analysis but by stimulating memories and feelings. History offers many examples of inspiring figures whose mystical experiences somehow ennobled them and whose teachings are capable of transforming our lives. Science and rationality are methods of gaining knowledge through analysis. What about methods that rely on synthesis such as intuition, inspiration, and revelation?

Neurotheology is a field of neuroscience that asks, what are the neural correlates of spiritual and mystical experience? Can these synthetic rather than analytical methods of knowing be shown to be the result of natural pathways in the brain? Is the apparent meaningfulness of intuition due to a common human response to the activation of brain circuits? Can the experience of the divine be explained as the triggering of a particular neurological process? In other words, can the determined atheist show that methods of seeking knowledge other than rational analysis can be explained as biochemical phenomena?

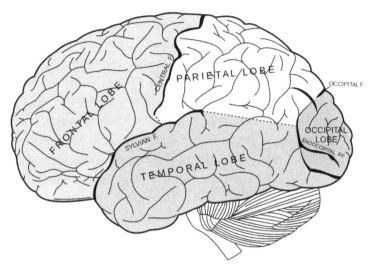

Figure 1. The different lobes of the cerebral cortex: the occipital, the parietal, the temporal, and the frontal lobes. From *Gray's Anatomy of the Human Body*, 20th U.S. edition, 1918, public domain.

The Miracle of the Brain

We stand in awe of the universe with its one hundred billion galaxies, each with on average one hundred billion stars. We could be equally in awe of the human brain that is composed of one hundred billion neurons with trillions of connections called synapses. It is perhaps the most complex natural phenomenon we are aware of. The cerebral cortex of the brain is roughly divided into sections that specialize in particular functions. Problem solving and judgment are handled by the frontal lobes, sensation and location in space by the parietal lobes, visual function by the occipital lobes, and memory and hearing are the work of the temporal lobes (see fig. 1).

Within the cerebral cortex, we will be particularly interested in the thalamus and the limbic system. Nearly centrally located in the brain, the thalamus is a hub for all circuits carrying information being processed by the brain. It is involved in pain sensation, alertness, attention, and memory. The limbic system consists of organs below the thalamus including the hypothalamus, amygdala, hippocampus, and the cingulate gyri (see fig. 2). The limbic system is responsible for emotions, learning, and memory. The hypothalamus regulates some of the functions of the autonomic nervous system. The amygdala is the most sensitive organ in the brain and handles emotions, while the hippocampus deals with memory. We will also be interested in the brain stem, which is the master control for autonomic functions such as breathing, heart rate, wake and sleep cycles, and digestion.

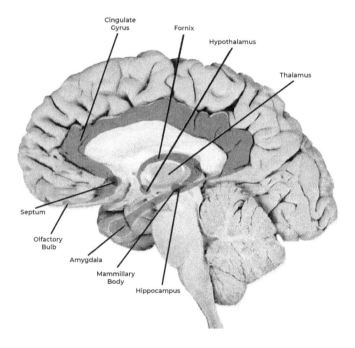

Figure 2. The limbic system. From https://en.wikiversity.org/wiki/File:Limbic_System.png; created by SoniaM2020, October 20, 2020. Licensed under Creative Commons Attribution-Share Alike 4.0 International.

The brain is divided into right and left hemispheres connected by a band of nerve fibers called the corpus callosum. All the features of the brain described above have their left and right brain versions except the hypothalamus and the brain stem. The left brain controls the right side of the body and the right brain the left side. Although the two sides of the brain seem symmetrical, there are differences that characterize each side. The left side is specialized for language, analytic thought, logic, and reasoning while the right side specializes in creativity, imagination, intuition, and feeling. In normal functioning, the two sides are integrated by the communication passing through the corpus callosum and we experience a single personality. For those whose corpus callosum has been severed by injury or for medical reasons, there is evidence of two separate personalities that respond differently to the same stimuli. For these rare cases, as long as both sides of the brain receive the same sensory input, it is difficult to distinguish the two personalities. If sensory input is blocked for one side of the brain, the different reactions of the two sides of the brain become clear.

Neurotheology Research

How can one make the connection between spiritual experiences and activity in the brain? Early indications came from studies of patients with temporal lobe epilepsy. Behavioral neurologist Norman Geschwind noted that some temporal lobe epilepsy subjects exhibited signs of religiosity following seizures. Those observed behaviors called the Geschwind syndrome include a tendency for compulsive writing, intense religious feelings, and philosophical interests. These symptoms within the context of the syndrome are clearly pathological. Some scientists have speculated that temporal lobe epilepsy led to the visions of Joan of Arc as well as the revelations of prophets such as Moses, Jesus, Saint Paul, and Muhammad.

Some decades earlier, the Canadian neurosurgeon Wilder Penfield sought to relieve through surgery the suffering of temporal lobe epilepsy patients from frequent seizures. His treatment removed tissue that might trigger seizures. Before the surgery, he used electrodes to stimulate the surrounding tissue to try to identify sensitive areas and avoid damage to body functions. In this way, he was able to map the location of sensory and motor responses from different parts of the body primarily on the parietal lobe. This mapping is called the homunculus or miniature person (see fig. 3).

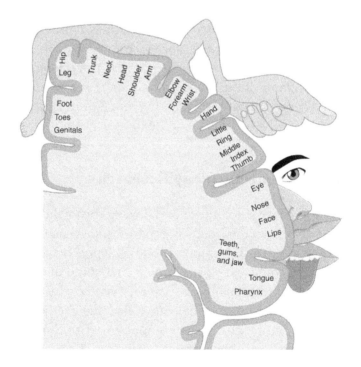

Figure 3. A 2-D cortical sensory homunculus. Image created by OpenStax College, Anatomy & Physiology, Connexions website. Access for free at https://openstax.org/books/anatomy-and-physiology/pages/1-introduction.

Penfield found that stimulation of the temporal lobes could stimulate recall of memories in vivid detail. He also found that such stimulation could produce visual and auditory hallucinations and even out-of-body experiences.

The God Helmet

Impressed by these experiments using electrical stimulation, Dr. Michael Persinger, a behavioral psychologist, decided to explore magnetic fields generated in the brain and found that he could detect fluctuating patterns in the temporal lobes. He was able to record and reproduce those patterns and feed them back into the brain by using a helmet that generated weak fields. He reasoned that by feeding back the magnetic field patterns generated by the brain, he would stimulate the organs in the brain that had produced the fields and correlate their activity with the experience reported by the subject. The device became popularly known as the God helmet.

Todd Murphy, an associate of Dr. Persinger, described the findings of a decade of research with the God helmet in *Sacred Pathways: The Brain's Role in Religious and Mystical Experiences.* Patterns were recorded from different parts of the limbic system and played back through the helmet to the right or left side of the brain. The subjects reported experiencing spiritual phenomena such as strong impressions of the presence of another being in the room, out-of-body experiences, and vague impressions of the experience of God. Dr. Persinger remarked,

> I suspect most people would call these "vague-all-around-me" sensations "God" but they are reluctant to employ the label in a laboratory. The implicit is obvious. If the equipment and the experiment produced the presence that was God, then the extra personal,

unreachable and independent characteristics of the God definition may be challenged.[1]

Todd Murphy notes in his book that the God helmet subjects' experiences match some of the stages of the near-death experience (NDE). His list of NDE stages includes:

1. Out-of-body experience
2. Passing through a tunnel
3. Encountering a bright light and dead relatives
4. The being of Light
5. The life review
6. A transcendent experience
7. The point of no return

Not all of these experiences are reported for every NDE. The first two stages are most commonly experienced. To elaborate on the meaning of each stage, for example, the first stage, an out-of-body experience, is often reported as looking down on one's body and seeing the medical procedures that are happening as doctors attempt to revive the unconscious patient. The being of Light is often described as feeling overwhelmingly loved and accepted. Sometimes the being of Light is described as God or a religious figure such as Jesus. The life review generally happens quickly, highlighting those experiences, good and bad, that epitomize what one has learned in one's life. Then follows the transcendent experience, a feeling of oneness with all and an impression that all questions have been answered and all knowledge is freely available. Finally, one encounters a threshold. If the threshold is crossed, one feels there is no turning back. Before crossing, there is an opportunity to return to life for some purpose that seems clear at that moment but later is difficult to recall.

1. Todd Murphy, *Sacred Pathways* (self-published, 2015), 115.

Research has been conducted to try to determine which of these stages might be due to cultural impressions. A study of Japanese NDEs did not turn up an experience of life review. The Light encountered in the fourth stage was not experienced as a being, but rather as a soothing light that brought peace. The study's authors acknowledge that a small number of NDEs were available, and a larger sample might turn up the missing experiences.[2]

Murphy assumes that the experiences represented by the stages of an NDE are a template for the whole gamut of spiritual experiences reported by mystics and the general population. His assumption is based on the idea that sacred pathways exist in the brain that are activated generally by spiritual experiences and culminate at the time of death. He attempts to trace those sacred pathways from experiments with the God helmet that correlate stimulation of parts of the limbic system with spiritual experiences of the subjects. His understanding of these pathways is based on general neurological knowledge about the functioning of the limbic system.

To more easily explain the working of the limbic system, he presents a simplified version of how that system works. In reality, the limbic system is not as isolated as he presents it but is interconnected in complicated ways especially with the cortex or surface layers of the frontal and temporal lobes. The limbic system includes the amygdala, hippocampus, and caudate nucleus (see fig. 4).

2. Masayuki Ohkado and Bruce Grayson, "A Comparative Analysis of Western and Japanese NDEs," *Journal of Near-Death Studies* 32, no. 4 (Summer 2014): 187–98.

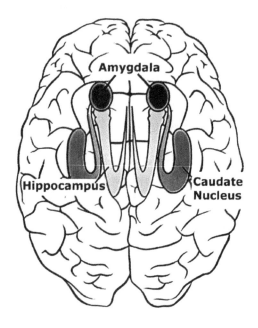

Figure 4. A simplified version of the brain's limbic system. Image from Murphy, *Sacred Pathways*, 61.

Generally, the limbic system is the emotional center of the brain. Its functions are specialized according to the characteristics of the left and right versions of its organs.

The most sensitive part of the limbic system is the amygdala. The left amygdala when stimulated is involved in experiences of joy, happiness, elation, and bliss. It is also connected to the language centers on the left side of the brain. Experiences linked with the left amygdala can be articulated. By contrast, the right amygdala is associated with feelings of fear, anxiety, and depression. As the right side of the brain lacks language centers, experiences on that side are felt rather than articulated.

Collecting and accessing memories is one of the chief functions of the hippocampus. Verbal memories are stored by the left hippocampus and contribute to our sense of self.

Nonverbal memories are accessed by the right hippocampus. The right hippocampus is also responsible for inner imagery as in dreams. It seems to be the primary place in the brain where theta waves are produced. Theta waves are associated with the intention to act, rapid eye movement (REM) sleep, and states of meditation. Spatial perception and balance are functions of the right hippocampus.

The caudate nucleus coordinates the body's state of resistance or readiness for felt emotional states. Its left side relates to joy and language. Its right side supports arousal as well as relaxation which can sink into depression and lethargy. Interactions between the right caudate nucleus and the right hippocampus can create calm as experienced in meditation and push away fear associated with the right amygdala.

The right and left parts of each organ and the organs of the limbic system themselves are connected by nerve tissue that allows them to communicate and influence each other.

The Neurological Sense of Self

Where does the sense of self come from? The social sense of self relies heavily on the language ability of the left side of the brain. This social self is the conditioned sense of self. We take in impressions of how we think others perceive us, and we imagine how our own impression of our body, mind, speech, and emotional life is received and judged by others. Our confidence and self-esteem are shaped by these impressions. The integrated impression we identify as our self is continually reinforced by verbalizing it through our inner speech and our thoughts.

Actually, the two sides of the brain each have a different personality. Generally speaking, the left-brain personality is logical and objective while the right-brain personality tends to be creative and subjective. As long as communication between the left and right sides is intact, we are able to integrate their two personalities into one. The left side of the brain is dominant. It has the major influence over who we think we are because it continually reinforces our notions of self through internal dialogue. If the corpus callosum that links the two hemispheres is severed, the right and left personalities or "selves" can be observed as functioning distinctly.

The neuroanatomist Jill Bolte Taylor, during a stroke that incapacitated the left side of her brain, directly experienced the personality of the right side of the brain. She describes her experience in *My Stroke of Insight*.[3] When the continual subvocal chattering of the left side of the brain subsided, she felt peace and euphoria. Memories of the past and imaginings of the future faded away and she felt splendidly awake in the present moment. Her sense of self became fluid rather than solid. She no longer felt like a distinct individual separated from everything external. Rather, she felt connected to all. The defensive protective stance of the ego faded, and she felt safe despite the urgency of the situation as she realized she was in the midst of a life-threatening stroke. She was able to remain conscious and retain somewhat detailed memories of what happened as the stroke developed. In the process of recovery, she found she could hold on to the experience of her right brain personality while she consciously integrated it with her returning left brain functioning. Her description of the experience of right brain consciousness is similar to reported experiences of meditators and mystics.

We have an idea of the way the self is experienced when the left side of the brain is dominant and when it is offline through injury or pacification. Many sensations go into the sense of self. Scientists have asked, what is the binding factor that integrates all these sensations into what is sensed as single and whole? A particular wave pattern called a gamma

3. Jill Bolte Taylor, *My Stroke of Insight* (New York: Penguin Random House, 2008).

wave is observed in conscious subjects to run from the thalamus, through which are threaded all sensory paths, across the brain from front to back, at a frequency of forty times per second. In dreamless sleep and other circumstances when a subject is unconscious this pattern is absent. Evidence suggests that consciousness and the sense of self are linked, and that gamma waves somehow bind the diverse contributions that make up the impression of a self.

Murphy points out that when one tries to focus on the sense of self, it proves to be beyond one's grasp. Although it can be sensed in a vague and conceptual way, focusing on it only makes it more obscure. He notes that those who experience hallucinations also report the elusive nature of impressions during those events. Various kinds of hallucinations occur in temporal lobe epilepsy; the sense of self also seems to arise from the temporal lobes. Could the sense of self then be a type of hallucination? This would confirm the Buddhist teaching that there is no separate self. Murphy thinks that the hallucination of the self has a function in binding the many impressions we receive and allowing us to respond in an integrated way.

> Our idea is that the sense of self is a hallucination, a functional hallucination with a job to do. Its function seems to be to unite everything that happens to the organism we live in, both from within and without, into a single phenomenon that can communicate with the rest of our bodies and minds. The sense of self is both a phenomenon and a sense. It responds to other phenomena in much the same way as the standard five senses respond to input. You could say that the self responds to vision as vision responds to colors.[4]

4. Murphy, *Sacred Pathways*, 268.

Based on this notion of self as a hallucination, Murphy has an explanation for the sensed presence of another often reported in the God helmet sessions. The magnetic influence of the helmet quiets the dominant left side of the brain considerably. The unfamiliar right-side personality is then projected out as an unseen presence. One feels it in the room as a distinct entity. When the projection occurs in a spiritual state it might seem to be a visitation by a spiritual presence such as an angel, a prophet, or God.

A Neurological Explanation of Mystical Experience

Murphy's explanation of powerful inner experience is based on his understanding of the way the limbic system works when pushed to an extreme. Suppose the limbic system is activated by strong emotional stimulation. As the amygdala is the most sensitive part of the limbic system, it will receive an impulse of energy.

Murphy takes the death experience, assuming it is characterized by the NDE stages, as a template for all mystical experiences. Typically, approaching the experience of death involves fear and anxiety. There may be pain and depression. This kind of emotion is associated with the right amygdala. If the right caudate nucleus is also stimulated, the energy of depression turns toward despair. Such an amplification further stimulates the right amygdala, raising the ante to feelings of anguish. When the level of stimulation of the right amygdala reaches a threshold, its energy spills over to the left amygdala in a movement called interhemispheric intrusion. Suddenly feelings of despair and anguish give way to feelings of bliss and contentment, associated with stimulation of the left amygdala. As the right hippocampus is still activated, feelings of sudden enlightenment are accompanied by a sense of deep insight, as the right hippocampus is where meaning is discovered. If the left caudate nucleus becomes stimulated, the sense of silent knowing can become verbalized along with a feeling of passionate love.

When the right amygdala dumps its energy into the left amygdala across the connecting neural bridge, because of the intensity of the energy flow, inhibitory synapses are pruned making future flow from right to left easier. According to Murphy, this accounts for the transformation that can occur in powerful spiritual openings. Since the brain has been altered to pass more easily from negative emotional states into peaceful or contented ones, the illuminated person functions in life more effortlessly.

Interhemispheric intrusion is meant to explain the stages one goes through at death as reported by those who have had near-death experiences as well as mystical experiences that replicate one or more of the NDE stages. To support the idea that mystical openings happen in this way, Murphy examines the stories of historical figures who have had such experiences.

For example, the night before his enlightenment, the Buddha is said to have struggled with the temptress Mara. This legend may refer to psychological struggles the Buddha was having with a self or ego desperate to stay alive. The victory of no-self over self, according to Murphy, would have signified interhemispheric intrusion, the lighting up of the left amygdala and the pruning of the bridge between the amygdalae. The story of Eckhart Tolle's enlightenment has a similar motif. For years, he had been suffering from a feeling of despair as well as disillusionment with the world and with himself. The turmoil peaked around his twenty-ninth birthday. As it reached an unbearable intensity, a question arose in his mind, "If I can't live with myself, am I actually two rather than one? Who is the one who can't live with me?" This thought triggered some of the signs of an NDE—he felt himself pulled into a dark tunnel and then fell into a void. Everything changed and when he awoke, he found he was experiencing stable peace and contentment. For the Indian mystic Ramana Maharshi, there is a similar story. As a youth, a sudden anxiety attack left him feeling he was about to die. He examined the experience by imitating death of the body and had a sudden realization that the body was animated by a living spirit that would not die.

Murphy acknowledges that not all experiences of enlightenment follow this pattern of a dark negative state followed by a sudden reversal into elation. He believes that some people are inherently sensitive and can have an awakening of the left amygdala without interhemispheric intrusion. However, he feels he has found the best scientific explanation for the moment for religious or spiritual transformation, and that future studies will build on this hypothesis. He concludes:

> Some religious thinkers will denounce this book. However, the advance of science into our cultures is a trend that can't be reversed. Science is now a part of basic education no matter how rudimentary, in every country on earth; even the poorest of them. An understanding of spirituality that agrees with science will inevitably supplant religion whose only basis is in traditional scriptures. The beauty of traditional religion will always inspire, and its teachings will remain good for people. However, in the present era, only science can offer explanations that will endure, even though those explanations can and will change.[5]

The work of Dr. Persinger and Todd Murphy has been criticized by other scientists. Some have tried to reproduce the God helmet research and haven't found the same results. Some say that the reports of the subjects can be accounted for by suggestibility and that double-blind procedures were not followed. Others claim that the weak magnetic fields pro-

5. Ibid., 398.

duced by the God helmet would not be able to penetrate the skull and influence the brain. Although Murphy has countered these complaints, the research remains controversial.

A Different Explanation of NDEs

In *The Spiritual Doorway in the Brain: A Neurologist's Search for the God Experience*, neurologist Kevin Nelson persuasively explains the phenomena of the NDE as a brain stem malfunction he calls REM intrusion. There are three conditions of consciousness—the awake state, REM dreaming, and non-REM dreamless sleep. Regulation of these states of consciousness is the work of the brain stem. The states are usually separated by an on-or-off switch. Normally there is little mixing of these states. Of course, everyone experiences a borderline state when descending into dreams or emerging from them. Usually, this is a smooth transition. There are, however, conditions in which this transition is disrupted. In narcolepsy, for example, the switch over to the REM state can happen repeatedly and unexpectedly. Seeing that some of the phenomena of an NDE can be experienced when the brain stem switch is not working properly, Nelson wondered,

> If REM consciousness sparks the near-death experience, and since not everyone has a near-death experience in crisis, maybe the arousal brain in people who have these special experiences predisposes them to blend REM and wakeful consciousness. Some people, because of the way their brains work, might be susceptible to blending REM and waking consciousness, not only during the crisis of being near death but at other times as well.[6]

6. Kevin Nelson, *The Spiritual Doorway in the Brain* (New York: Dutton, Penguin Group, 2011), 338.

To test this hypothesis, Nelson's research team questioned fifty-five subjects who had reported NDEs and a control group of fifty-five subjects with matching demographics who had never experienced an NDE. The team used a standardized questionnaire to examine borderland experiences such as lucid dreaming, feelings of paralysis upon waking, seeing visions, hearing sounds, and hallucinating, other than from NDEs. The results showed that REM intrusion phenomena were two and a half times more likely for NDE subjects than for the control group.

Nelson lays the groundwork for his hypothesis step-by-step. What conditions are likely to precede an NDE? With fainting and heart disturbances, typically blood flow to the brain is significantly reduced. Some physicians have reported that the brain shuts down in NDEs. If blood flow to the brain is reduced by 70 percent, the subject loses consciousness, but the brain can remain uninjured in that condition for hours. Even if blood flow to the brain stops altogether, the brain can continue to function for ten seconds. Afterward, although the brain will malfunction, it can continue for several minutes before death of the cells sets in.

Researchers who have studied fainting in the lab discovered that 60 percent of subjects had visual hallucinations in the unconscious or borderland state before waking up. The kinds of hallucinations reported were comparable with NDE reports. For example, when blood flow to the eyes is restricted, peripheral vision is reduced producing the impression of a tunnel. Tunnel vision is often reported by those who experience fainting.

Another feature of NDEs can also be reproduced in the lab. Olaf Blanke, a neurologist in Switzerland, made a discovery while following up on the work of Wilder Penfield with temporal lobe epileptics. Preparing to surgically remove tissue in the brain that was triggering seizures, Blanke found that by stimulating a point deep in the boundary between the temporal and parietal lobes (the temporoparietal bound-ary) his subject experienced being lifted out of her body. By successively applying and removing the stimulus, he found that the sense of having an out-of-body experience could be turned on and off like a switch. Near the temporoparietal boundary lies the cortical region responsible for vestibular orientation. When the area is stimulated, orientation to the body is disturbed and we have the sensation of rising, of viewing the body from above, which presumably is supplied by imagination.

Disturbance of the temporoparietal boundary can also produce the sensation of another's presence. Nelson spec-ulates that a sensed presence can be enhanced by memory and imagination.

Next, Nelson turns to the function of the brain stem and its link with the limbic system, both of which are involved in the brain's arousal system. The arousal system manages the alertness or passiveness of consciousness through the re-lease of the chemicals noradrenaline for stimulation or ace-tylcholine for pacification. In the fight-or-flight response, the brain releases noradrenaline to enhance our vigilance, and the body releases adrenaline to maximize our physical abil-ity to respond. In the relaxation response triggered by deep relaxation or meditation, the brain releases acetylcholine to bring about a feeling of peace and contentment and release of stress. Nelson makes a connection between the immi-nence of death, which in the case of NDEs is often brought about by a traumatic injury, and the fight-or-flight response. He speculates that when the injury is too traumatic or death seems unavoidable, the relaxation response takes over and the subject is spared unnecessary suffering.

The limbic system also engages the reward system of the brain that earmarks what we like, our preferences, and de-sires. Our notion of a spiritual reward, such as the comforts of heaven or a merging with unconditional love, may also be stored in the limbic system and may influence the playing out of each NDE.

The question remains of how these reactions and stored memories can be integrated in the narrative of the NDE in a convincing and consistent way. For an answer, Nelson turns to REM sleep. How does REM sleep happen? Electrical waves, called ponto-geniculo-occipital waves, are generated by the pons in the brain stem. They travel upward to the lateral geniculate nuclei attached to the thalamus. All visual input from the eyes passes through the lateral geniculate nuclei and then to the occipital lobe where visual input is processed. The waves from the pons also pass through the lateral geniculate nuclei and then proceed to the visual center of the brain. Although visual input in this case is not coming from the eyes, the activation of the occipital lobe causes an impression as though viewing something external, producing rapid eye movement. The emotional content of dreams comes from the limbic system. Memories are supplied by the hippocampus.

Another important part of the brain that contributes to dreams is the dorsolateral prefrontal cortex. This part of the cortex is responsible for the executive functioning of the brain. It organizes thought, information, and emotions. During REM sleep, this part of the cortex is inactive. This accounts for the disorganized and irrational changes typical of dreams. If the dorsolateral prefrontal cortex does not turn off, we are able to be aware we are dreaming, an experience called lucid dreaming. This is a persistent borderland state mixing REM sleep and waking consciousness. Because executive functioning is present, lucid dreams seem more real than ordinary dreams. The imagery is experienced as though one is awake with the same clarity, vividness, and realness. The gamma waves we considered earlier, running from front to back, which may indicate a binding factor that consolidates a sense of self, are generally turned off during

REM sleep but come back on in lucid dreaming. This adds to the feeling of reality and continuity with everyday life.

As noted earlier, there is a switch in the brain stem that normally is set either to REM sleep or waking consciousness. Within that switch, there is a component that moves toward waking consciousness when activated. This component is triggered by the fight-or-flight response and stimulates the release of noradrenaline to enhance alertness. If the stimulus for flight-or-fight becomes too extreme, as mentioned above, when pain is too great or escape too remote, this component shuts down, stopping the release of noradrenaline and allowing the parasympathetic system to dominate with acetylcholine, bringing about peace, passivity, and sleepiness. This mechanism supports Nelson's speculation about how surrender comes about in the dying process in the case of trauma or imminent death.

What about the light that is seen at the end of the tunnel in NDEs and the brilliant light that seems to radiate peace and acceptance? For the light at the end of the tunnel, Nelson suggests a connection with the remnant of light that continues to come through the eyes as the peripheral vision shuts down due to lack of blood flowing to the eyes. Another source of light is produced during REM sleep when the eyes are closed, and no outside light is coming in. Nelson does not explain why the near-death experience of light would be blindingly bright as is often reported.

Finally, the experience of warmth, safety, and unconditional love described in NDEs, Nelson labels rapture. As mentioned earlier, rapturous experiences may be triggered by the release of acetylcholine by the parasympathetic system during the stress of an NDE. (The reward system in the brain is triggered by the presence of acetylcholine.) Nelson believes the experience of light at the end of the tunnel is linked to REM consciousness, which also stimulates the brain's reward system. Therefore, Nelson speculates that the reward system is stimulated during NDEs bringing about feelings of bliss.

To summarize, Nelson presents powerful arguments to support the idea that NDEs represent a particular dysfunction of the brain stem's REM switch. He believes that NDEs are limited to those who also experience such things as lucid dreams, fainting, paralysis upon waking, visions, and hallucinations. Stages of an NDE can be explained as the result of the mixing of REM consciousness and waking consciousness, and therefore, general conclusions about the nature of death and the question of life after death cannot be drawn from the accounts of those who have gone through one or more NDEs.

On the subject of the spiritual aspect of NDEs or mystical experiences, Nelson admits science has very little to go on. By mystical experience, he means a loss of a sense of self and a feeling of unity with all. He points to the results of an experiment to map the brain areas activated by spiritual experience. Mario Beauregard and Vincent Paquette ran magnetic resonance imaging scans on a group of Carmelite nuns who were asked to relive during the scans their most intense mystical experiences. The nuns were clear that simply recalling their experiences didn't propel them back into the actual states they had been in. Furthermore, although the scans showed activity, it was spread out over the brain and didn't reveal any obvious pattern. Andrew Newberg, studying brain activity in Tibetan Buddhist meditators and Franciscan nuns, found a similarly wide distribution in the brain's response.

Nelson feels that attempts to explain spiritual phenomena scientifically or spiritually need to be approached with caution because of the all-too-clever ability of the mind to concoct rationalizations.

Do these cold, hard clinical facts suck the divine nectar from our spiritual lives? My answer is an empathic NO! We are poised on the threshold of a new era that holds tremendous promise for a new level of spiritual exploration.

I urge caution, however. We need to be wary of our left hemisphere, the explainer and confabulator in our brains. It has led us astray so many times in the past, giving us a plethora of gods, including a mathematical god, to explain the natural world around us. The left hemisphere has given others the reasons to explain away our spiritual essence, often with hubris. It's unlikely that the left hemisphere today has changed its basic nature after more than one hundred thousand years of evolution. It is all too willing to look for natural and supernatural explanations.[7]

NDEs: Evidence from Personal Accounts

In another approach to investigating NDEs, Dr. Jeffrey Long, an oncologist with a fascination for NDEs, founded the Near Death Experience Research Foundation in 1998. He set up an online survey website and invited those who have experienced NDEs to submit their personal accounts and complete a detailed questionnaire. The questionnaire establishes the circumstances of their NDE and asks specific questions about how they experienced the identified NDE stages. Over 4,000 subjects responded providing the largest database of NDE testimony ever assembled. The sample is culturally diverse with submissions in over twenty languages. Long summarized the results of his studies of this database in his book *God and the Afterlife*.[8] Comments in the book apply to a sample

7. Ibid., 432.
8. Jeffrey Long, *God and the Afterlife* (New York: HarperCollins, 2016).

of 1,100 subjects selected sequentially from reports submitted over a three-year period.

Long is impressed by the content of the NDEs more than the stages such as out-of-body experiences, tunnel vision, encountering a bright light, and so on. Nelson and other neurologists offer explanations for the mechanisms that might underlie out-of-body experiences or tunnel vision. Long's study compares the vividness of NDEs to the realness of lucid dreams, the result of a mixing of REM sleep and waking consciousness. Long calls attention to the heightening of the senses reported in NDEs that make them seem "realer than real." Presumably, the content of lucid dreams, like other dreams, is fed by the imagination working on stored memories, often expressed in symbolic ways. What Nelson's explanation doesn't account for is the extraordinary similarity of the reported heightened experiences for many NDE respondents. Why would the proposed explanations lead to nearly the same experience for each reporter? If failing blood supply to the brain and eyes can account for an out-of-body experience with awareness that one is dying, and for the impression of passing through a tunnel, why would imagination plus memories always call up an encounter with a brilliant light that conveys a feeling of unconditional love? Dreamlike memory could conjure feelings of being loved by parents, a human lover, or a variety of past experiences of love, but instead the encounter is typically affirmed as ineffable, as an experience of merging with the all-encompassing, as meeting the overwhelming power of love.

Long is so impressed with the consistency and richness of the large collection of reports he assembled that he feels they offer a transformational discovery that could affect our cultural view of death and radically improve the quality of our lives.

Our situation regarding NDEs is similar to the way humanity learned of exotic lands during the ancient era of exploration. After sailors returned from long voyages and wrote their accounts, scholars would survey multiple accounts from different voyagers, discern where they agreed or disagreed, and come up with the most likely descriptions of the geography, culture, rituals, and traditions of a particular exotic land. We are in a similar position today when it comes to the world of the afterlife.[9]

Long takes a special interest in reports of the encounter with a bright light. Some describe this encounter as a meeting with God. To investigate this phenomenon, Long sent out a follow-up survey with questions about this encounter. In this case, his sample included 420 reports. Roughly equal numbers in his sample (about 40 percent each) said their experience either did, or did not, give them an awareness of the existence of God. The remainder weren't sure. Comparing belief in God before the experience and after, he found that 40 percent believed before and 73 percent believed after the experience. In this sample, the average time that had transpired since the NDE was twenty years, so the change in belief was persistent. Concerning prior religious affiliation, responders divided themselves equally between liberal, moderate, and conservative. Those divisions didn't change significantly from before the experience to twenty years later. However, in personal reports, respondents said their religious views considerably broadened. They expressed tolerance for different beliefs, feeling that their personal beliefs were more meaningful to them than their experience in places of worship, as well as disagreement with doctrines that represented God as judging or condemning. In their experience, God

9. Ibid., 2–3.

was totally accepting and loving. They questioned the use of the word God because they found it too limiting. Although they said their experiences were ineffable, they felt the love they experienced had transformed their lives.

Two typical testimonies:

> This presence didn't tell me it was God—that was my later determination—we try to ascribe labels to things that shouldn't have labels. Anyway, this intense energy force wanted to be with me and that was all I cared about at that time.
>
> I had the awareness that a spiritual force exists that is all of us combined, not separate. If the word "God" is used, then God is all of us.[10]

Their accounts of the experiences they called "God" matched what Nelson called the mystical experience, an absorption into oneness with a sense of love and great power. Long comments,

> For many NDErs, what they encountered was so different from their prior understanding of God that their questioning of the term God is understandable. What we can say is that in NDEs there is a consistent encounter with a loving and compassionate intelligence. What NDErs learn about the nature of this entity is probably more important than what earthly terms they use to describe this entity—whether the term is God, the One, the Order, Light, or Supreme Being. All these terms point to what I call God in this book for lack of a better and widely understood English-language term.[11]

10. Ibid., 176–78.
11. Ibid., 180.

What does Long have to say about the evidence of REM intrusion as an explanation of NDEs? Nelson's key evidence came from his survey of fifty-five NDE subjects who indicated they had a history of REM intrusions such as lucid dreaming, paralysis upon waking, or hallucinations. Long was actually involved in securing the subjects for Nelson's study. He points out that 40 percent of the NDE subjects reported no prior experience of REM intrusion experiences. Further, it wasn't established whether those who did report REM intrusion experiences had them before or after the NDE. It might be expected that after a dramatic and life changing NDE, a subject might be more prone to experiencing REM intrusion or to paying attention to such experiences while others might be more likely to dismiss them.

Long has written another book, *Evidence of the Afterlife*, in which he presents extensive evidence for the reality of NDEs.[12] For example, he cites twenty-three NDEs that occurred under general anesthesia, during which no conscious brain activity can occur. Yet, the reported experiences of those twenty-three NDEs do not differ from those of other NDEs. Another study compared the out-of-body experience impressions of patients who had suffered cardiac arrest. Those who did not have NDEs reported confused and inaccurate impressions of resuscitation efforts, while the impressions of those who did have NDEs were clear, logical, and accurate even in details.

Conclusion

Neurotheology is in its infancy as a science. Although some progress has been made, many of the ideas presented here remain speculative. Andrew Newberg has great hopes for the field and feels it will make major contributions to medicine and to quality of life in the future. Even if science can trace

12. Jeffrey Long, *Evidence of the Afterlife* (New York: HarperCollins, 2010).

the pathways in the brain that underlie spiritual or mystical experiences, the challenge that remains is similar to what is called "the hard problem" in the field of consciousness. How does one make the leap from neuronal mechanisms to the content of experience? This is the problem Dr. Long highlights in his advocacy for the meaningfulness of NDE narratives.

3

Rationalism and Other Ways of Knowing

IF SCIENCE HAS not been able to explain away alternative ways of understanding and gaining insight such as intuition, inspiration, and revelation, then should we reconsider ideas of religion and the existence of God based on these sources of knowledge? What is revelation? A simple description of revelation would be that it is the visionary experience of a prophet, the revealing of God's message to humanity. A skeptic would question whether this is a reliable experience. Is it hallucinatory behavior? From our modern understanding of the phenomena of mental illness, one might wonder whether prophetic revelation is a particularly grandiose version of delusional thinking. But then, one would have to assume that millions of followers were deluded by the teachings of a prophet while a handful of scholars alone had the discrimination to avoid being taken in. One could then question who it was that was being grandiose!

Let's explore a little further what revelation might mean. We are familiar with rational thinking. This is the preferred and reliable way of thinking approved by science. Another form of understanding is intuition. Although scientists might be cautious about intuition, it has played a key role in important scientific discoveries. Intuition comes as a sudden insight or a hunch. Intuition is a common way of thinking in everyday life. We don't typically take time to think things through rationally and logically, unless we have to make an important decision. In the bustle of daily life, we are much more likely to operate on intuition, or a feeling for what is needed. We might think of the brain as the place of reasoning and the heart as the place of feeling. We might be more likely to function in the moment from the heart. Typically, the heart is seen as watching out for our own interest. If, however, our heart expands and we are lifted to a more generous feeling, intuition may be raised to inspiration. This feeling is known especially by artists and comes as a gift. It comes in response to a mood of expansion or elation. If our mood becomes elated by immersion in feelings of sacredness to the extent that thoughts of self fade away, inspiration may turn into revelation. While the artist may feel that inspiration has come from a muse, the one who receives revelation feels the gift has come from a spiritual source.

The great prophets such as Moses, Jesus, and Muhammad felt they were instructed through revelation to serve humanity, to raise the consciousness of humanity to a higher level of compassion and generosity. Their version of religion was not a teaching to explain how the world works. They didn't offer supernatural explanations for natural events. What they chiefly offered was a way to live with dignity, honor, and consideration for others.

Rationalism and Western Theology

How is it that in our time the idea of God has been challenged on the playing field of rationalism? How did we wind up with a rational critique of the existence of God starting from prophetic revelations that offered humanity a message of hope and relief from suffering? Karen Armstrong has traced the development of ideas about God in the traditions of Judaism, Christianity, and Islam in *A History of God*.[1] She earmarks the influence of Greek philosophy on all three religions.

It is tempting to say that the impressive and inspiring philosophies of Plato and Aristotle catalyzed efforts in each religion to bring rationalism to bear in formulating doctrines or dogmas. However, I believe the Greek influence is a bit more complex. Plato's famous metaphor of the cave, suggesting that humans see only shadows on the wall of a brilliant reality outside the cave consisting of "ideas" or archetypal qualities, is a mystical rather than a rational conception. However, his stories about the method of Socrates, who guided philosophical discussions by asking penetrating questions, affirms a rational and logical way of investigation. Aristotle used rational and logical thinking as well as empirical methods to develop his theories about the world. He introduced the idea of the Unmoved Mover as God much like the God of Spinoza or Einstein, a God who has no interest in human affairs or even in the universe. Aristotle's God stood still and eternal beyond the chaos of the material world.

As each of the three Abrahamic religions became the dominant cultural matrix for its sphere of influence, the study of nature's outer life in the form of physics, astronomy, psychology, and philosophy was thoroughly mixed with the theology of nature's inner life. Under the influence of Greek rationalism, especially of Aristotle's prescientific reliance on the evidence of the senses, religious thinkers sought to make the rational and empirical observations of nature conform to religious ideas about God the Creator and Controller of events. They adopted Plato's idea of God as the Good and Aristotle's idea that God is perfect and this world imperfect.

1. Karen Armstrong, *A History of God* (New York: Ballantine/Random House, 1993).

We are familiar with the drama played out in Christian culture. The attempt to impose on nature a design consistent with notions derived from inner realizations led to a theory of crystalline spheres in the heavens that came crashing down with the insight of Copernicus and the observations of Kepler as well as the discoveries of Galileo. As the scientific revolution accelerated, study of nature increasingly shifted away from the umbrella of the Church. It became more secularized. Yet, the Church continued to resist new discoveries that challenged its rationalized notion of God. Even to the present day, a persistent movement of resistance to scientific advances such as neo-Darwinism continues among Christian believers.

Contrary to this attempt to rationalize God in each of the Abrahamic faiths, strong influences insisted God is beyond the grasp of the intellect, beyond human conception. But that does not mean that one cannot have an experience that convinces one of the reality of God. In Jewish circles, remembering the presence of God is emphasized. Its most accessible form is Shekinah, a feminine expression of the divine spirit. Shekinah presides over the most treasured and intimate ritual of Shabbat. Thus, the presence of God is integrated into the weekly celebration of the warmth of family life. A special time is set aside, an informal atmosphere of sacredness is invoked, the pleasures of a family meal are enjoyed, and the presence of God becomes associated with relaxation, love, joy, and Jewish identity. No rational concept of God is needed if the heart is open and a loving presence is felt.

In the Eastern Orthodox Church, the Cappadocians, Basil of Caesarea, Gregory of Nyssa, and Gregory of Nazianzus in the fourth century BCE argued that in Christianity, there is a public and a secret teaching. The public teaching is the familiar one drawn from the scriptures. One can only discover the secret teaching by preparing oneself and seeking its meaning in silence. About this secret teaching, Armstrong says,

[Basil] was simply calling attention to the fact that not all religious truth was capable of being expressed and defined clearly and logically. Some religious insights had an inner resonance that could only be apprehended by each individual in his own time during what Plato had called *theoria*, contemplation. Since all religion was directed toward an ineffable reality that lay beyond normal concepts and categories, speech was limiting and confusing.[2]

Attempts to understand God rationally are futile according to the faithful because the reality of God is beyond the capacity of the mind to grasp. However, the heart can experience things the mind cannot articulate. The simple and direct experience of presence or the experience that comes from stilling and opening the mind and heart can bring about a dramatic change in one's point of view, a knowing that is not rational or intellectual, that is difficult to explain.

The Christian mystic Meister Eckhart came close to affirming atheism when he said, "Man's last and highest parting is when, for God's sake, he takes leave of God." Eckhart was fond of making shocking statements. He spoke in the language of nondual thinking, of recognizing the oneness of God. From that perspective he called God nothing, by which he meant no individual thing but all possibility of every possible thing. If God is Nothing and we wish to get closer to God, then we must be prepared to make ourselves nothing. In the Islamic mystical tradition, there is a practice called *fana'* by which one seeks to forget oneself in the contemplation of a perfect Being. This is one way in which the secret of reality, the realization of God, may become an experience rather than a thought.

2. Ibid., 114.

Does the God of the Philosophers Shrink Away?

As the pursuit of knowledge in a Christian-dominated Western culture shifted from scholasticism under the umbrella of the Church to academic disciplines in secular university settings, philosophers began to challenge long-established ideas about God. The God of the Church was omnipotent and omniscient and at the same time loving and forgiving and also judging and condemning. We might anticipate that the philosopher's way of understanding God recedes historically from the theological view and tends toward atheism as scientific materialism comes to dominate intellectual thought. Let's look at the thinking of some prominent philosophers over the last three centuries to see if this is true.

Spinoza

We have already compared Einstein's "religion" with Baruch Spinoza's view of God as the source of the elegant laws of nature. What does a closer look at Spinoza's philosophy reveal about his idea of God? Spinoza felt that our outlook on life and our relationship with God is colored by personal self-interest. We project onto nature a power that we seek to mollify through prayer and actions that will bring us good fortune. This superstition persists despite the evident indifference of nature. We can free ourselves of this kind of self-serving ignorance by relying on the certainty and beauty of a mathematical understanding of nature. We can understand what happens in life through our efforts to uncover natural law by applying mathematics to empirical observations. When we have accepted that nature unfolds through laws that are irresistible, we will find peace.

Adopting the model of mathematics even for his philosophical thinking, Spinoza starts with a series of definitions and axioms. His definition of God is:

> By God, I understand Being absolutely infinite, that is to say, substance consisting of infinite attributes, each one of which expresses eternal and infinite essence.[3]

Spinoza uses the word "substance" to mean essence or beingness rather than material content. God is the simple essence of being behind every perceived outer object. God is the highest good, and our highest good is to seek knowledge of God. Intellect is the best part of our being, and we perfect our intellect through our love of God. This love is fulfilled in the satisfaction we gain by knowing the ways of God, not for our own self-interest or from fear of punishment.

We know God by seeing the beauty and orderliness of the laws of nature. Spinoza was accused of pantheism, reducing the unlimited nature of God to a presence underlying nature, but he denied it. Spinoza believed God is not limited to nature itself, although nature is animated by God. God is its substance or essential life. But God is infinite substance, while nature is finite and what Spinoza called mode.

> By substance, I understand that which is in itself and is conceived through itself; in other words, that, the conception of which does not need the conception of another thing from which it must be formed. . . .
>
> By mode, I understand the affections of substance, or that which is in another thing through which also it is conceived.[4]

---

3. Joseph Ratner, *The Philosophy of Spinoza* (Perennial Press e-book, 2016), 323.
4. Ibid., 322, 323.

Mode is an expression of the infinite attributes of God in their worldly form. God stands outside of nature yet permeates it. One could say that God as essence is the inner life of Reality and nature is its outer life.

For Spinoza, God is remote, not a personal God. In this way, Spinoza's God resembles the God of Einstein. And yet Spinoza goes further. God is a subtle essence that pervades and breathes life into what we perceive in the world. God is infinite, and inherent in God are the infinite attributes (akin to Plato's archetypal ideas). Our relationship with God through admiring worship is the source of our happiness. This relationship lifts us above our narrow and demeaning self-interest.

Kant

Through a process of reason and logic, can we arrive at an understanding of God or a proof of God's existence? Immanuel Kant examined the question of how we gain knowledge of the world through our senses in his *Critique of Pure Reason*. We don't perceive the world directly through our senses. There is an intermediate step in which sensory input is compiled into our perceptions of wholes. We see trees rather than leaves and branches and trunk separately. We perceive an idea of an object not the object-in-itself. We cannot know the essential nature of the object because it is covered over with a name and a form. But it is the essence of things that would reveal to us the nature of God. The essence of things is beyond the capacity of our minds to comprehend, as is the nature of God. If we can't perceive direct evidence for the nature of God, then the question of God's existence is mere speculation.

However, Kant felt he had uncovered another way to demonstrate the existence of God, albeit subjectively. In the *Critique of Practical Reason,* Kant examines the basis of our moral sense. He writes that we can't arrive at an understanding of right and wrong through our reason. There is no rational basis for our moral sense. However, he believes we have an innate feeling for what is right and wrong. It comes from the heart rather than the mind. He formulated a moral guideline that rises above self-interest: do not do what you would not want to see adopted into general practice. For example, you want to get away with a lie, but you would not want lying to become the norm, so you go with what would be best for all. He called this guideline the categorical imperative.

How does this analysis imply the existence of God? Kant felt that acting in a just way only makes moral sense if it entails a resolution of justice beyond this life. This implies a just Being who ensures that justice wins out in the end. Such an implication that God exists is not meant to be reasoned or logical. It is an observation about universal human behavior and psychology. It is tempting to say this boils down to a claim that our belief in a just God is what keeps us from living by the law of the jungle. If one were cynical, one could argue that we do indeed live by the law of the jungle. More in the spirit of what Kant was getting at, one could say that because we do have an innate sense of morality, we are reflecting an essential quality of justice that is an indication of God's existence.

It is interesting to observe that Kant was going beyond the scientific hubris of the day by suggesting that material objects have an essence or numinous existence, the thing-in-itself, that is beyond our ability to perceive. One could say Kant was pointing to a spiritual aspect of nature that complements its physical aspect.

Hegel

Like Kant, George Wilhelm Friedrich Hegel was interested in understanding the nature of reality. In his *Phenomenology of Spirit*, Hegel took on the ambitious goal of examining ways in which consciousness knows reality, and discovering—through the historical experience of each way of knowing—what he considered absolute knowing, the way in which consciousness knows itself. He set out to do this methodically, starting with the simplest way in which consciousness encounters reality. He called this beginning stage sense-certainty. This is a stage in which whatever consciousness encounters is taken at face value. Every object is unique. There is no grouping of objects by similarities. There is no analysis of the properties or characteristics of objects.

Hegel works his way through many stages of conscious knowing by using an ancient method he adapted in a particular way. In his version of the dialectical method, he posited a mode of conscious awareness, sense-certainty, as the first step. This presumption of a specific form of knowing is like the forming of a hypothesis in science. In the dialectical method, it is called the thesis. Experience of the limitations of human life ensures that the thesis will be flawed and lead to consideration of its opposite, which is called the antithesis. For the philosopher who is in love with knowing, experiencing the conflict between thesis and antithesis entails suffering. Philosophical knowledge grows through experience and acceptance of suffering. With passionate enthusiasm consciousness asserts a certainty about its current hypothesis. In the following quote, "shape" refers to a stage of conscious knowing.

> Consciousness strives repeatedly to transform its certainty into *truth*, that is, into a certainty that has *proved* itself. The movement of consciousness is tragic: learn-

ing is suffering. The more a shape struggles to transform mere certainty into truth, the more it suffers the consequences of its finitude, and generates the exact opposite of what it posited.[5]

The magic of the dialectical method is that a resolution arises from this conflict by the formation of a compromise between the two extremes. This resolution is called the synthesis. Hegel noted that its nature is to rise above thesis and antithesis. The synthesis then becomes the next rung on the ladder of the stages of conscious knowing.

Hegel is aware of the two forms of knowing, inward and outward or subjective and objective. This duality is the basis of the two forms of knowing that arise on each level. Sense-certainty in its first version is outward knowing.

Each object is sensed in the moment. However, sense-certainty has no capacity for process or change. So the problem of object continuity arises.

The antithesis to outward knowing is a corresponding inward knowing version of sense-certainty in which the "I" that knows is an immediate "I" with no distinguishing characteristics. It has no history or sense of continuity. While the "I" has memory, it has no sense of an enduring existence. Each moment, there is a unique "I." Logically, this doesn't work, because the notion of an infinite sequence of unique "I"s does not correspond to the experience of continuity.

The compromise or synthesis allows the subject and object to be universal rather than unique particulars. A universal subject or object is the same subject or object at different times. It has continuity of existence. Knowing a subject or object as universal is what Hegel calls perception. This is the second stage of knowing.

---

5. Peter Kalkavage, *The Logic of Desire* (Philadelphia: Paul Dry Books, Inc., 2007), 8.

In this way, Hegel passes through successive stages of conscious knowing: sense-certainty, perception, and understanding. Beyond this point, consciousness becomes self-consciousness.

> With the rise of self-consciousness, the Phenomenology becomes a different kind of book. It is now explicitly about man as spirit's self-manifestation. Man as consciousness was a detached theoretician. As self-consciousness, he desires and acts.[6]

Hegel continues on the dialectical path still climbing the ladder, but the path becomes more complicated. The next steps involve how self-consciousness desires and acts. At first, self-consciousness seeks to fulfill basic desires. In the antithesis, self-consciousness competes in what will lead to domination and submission. The rise of reason shapes the next stage. Science in the form of empirical knowing about nature on the one side competes with the pursuit of high ideals—as in the code of the knight—on the other. This stage is followed by an ethical stage in which one pays attention to either an inner code of right and wrong or an outer cultural code of mores. A religious stage follows in which appreciation of beauty becomes predominant. One finds beauty in the natural environment or in art which imagines an idealized form of beauty.

In seeking absolute knowing, Hegel arrives at what he considers the highest form of religion, Christianity. The nature of human consciousness is illustrated by the ideal of perfection as God the Father taking a human form, demonstrating that the ultimate nature of human consciousness is sacred. Hegel is not promoting Christianity per se but using it as an illustration of a philosophical truth.

6. Ibid., 91.

At various stages along the way, it was necessary to posit a Beyond and examine the relationship of human consciousness to the Beyond. At this highest stage, Hegel claims to have done away with the Beyond entirely. God is not beyond, but rather, is the ground of human consciousness. The dialectical process has by necessity grappled with the limitations of a dualistic perspective.

Hegel takes the last stage of religion one further step. Religion becomes absorbed into philosophical science. Anticipating nondual philosophy, Hegel resolves opposites, such as subject and object, ultimately by positing the source of self-consciousness as perfect, unlimited, and unified. It has no opposite. The life of Jesus can be pictured as an example of the true nature of reality. Spirit has its life through limited human lives. It escapes righteous rigidity through its recognition and acceptance of limitation and its willingness to forgive. It leaves a record of its emergence over the course of history through the progressive development of conscious awareness.

Hegel's brilliant analysis exposes many truths about human knowing and self-awareness. However, it is conceived in a European- and Christian-centric context and misses out on Eastern and Indigenous perspectives. He sees spirit revealing itself through European history and Christian revelation. How would his insights compare with a corresponding analysis of other world cultures and revelations?

Marx and Nietzsche

In the second half of the nineteenth century, the influence of scientific discovery continued to impact philosophy. From Hegel's focus on the burgeoning of spirit through the course of history, Karl Marx took a different lesson. He saw the decline of the divine right of kings and rising demands of the masses as a dramatic story of exploitation, injustice, and the awakening of the human spirit to its universal rights. For him, religion and the notion of God were used by the elite to pacify the workers. He denied the existence of God and called upon workers to take their destiny into their own hands. Heaven would no longer be a delayed gratification after a life of sacrifice but the outcome of a form of government that provided for all according to their needs. The benefits of industry and technology would be claimed for all.

Friedrich Nietzsche was moved by a similar impulse. Devoted to the Church as a youth, he became seriously disillusioned, and declared with distress, "God is dead. . . . And we have killed Him." He witnessed the turning from God and religion that was happening in intellectual circles and the erosion of religious authority. Like Marx, he felt that without God as Protector and Savior, it was now squarely up to the human being to take responsibility for the future. However, rather than turning to a political system as Marx did to provide for the needs of life, Nietzsche, influenced by Darwinian evolution, imagined a next step in human evolution to be a superman. Possibly influenced by his weak constitution and wish for greater masculinity, he pictured the superman in terms of social Darwinism—evolution will go in the direction of survival of the fittest. Consequently, he saw the Christian values of kindness, compassion, and forgiveness as weaknesses. Viewing nature without God as meaningless and uncaring, and calling for courage and heroism in taking responsibility for creating meaning in life, Nietzsche was an early existentialist.

Whitehead

Now we take a leap forward to the modern era. We might expect that philosophy has turned a corner and come fully into the service of scientific realism. In some ways, Alfred North Whitehead fits this expectation. Besides his work in philosophy, he was a noted mathematician and well acquainted with the science of his time, especially Einstein's theories of special and general relativity. He felt that philosophy and religion should be responsive to scientific discoveries and incorporate their ideas. To him, philosophy seemed to have become disengaged from science. He felt that as a discipline, philosophy should be useful to science.

Whitehead was not one to take received knowledge uncritically. He was critical of the way scientists simplify the objective world to make it easier to manage mathematically. For example, the use of the mathematical point as a location in space is an abstraction. Our common notion of an object is another abstraction. He coined the term "the fallacy of misplaced concreteness" to describe the error of treating abstractions as real. He felt that an understanding of our external reality should start from actual experience rather than abstractions. Reality should be described as a succession of events and relationships. Though he devoted most of his analysis to showing the inadequacy of the accepted way of viewing nature, he also laid the groundwork for a different way of viewing the world scientifically. That work continues to this day and has made a serious contribution to the field of artificial intelligence.

In *Process and Reality*, Whitehead set up a philosophy that clearly distinguishes between abstractions and actual experience. His intention was to formulate a description of reality that is organic rather than reductive and materialistic. Instead of matter being the basic substance whose properties define reality, he takes occasions of experience to be the substrate of reality. He divides occasions of experience into four grades: processes operating in a vacuum such as universal fields like gravity and electromagnetism, experiences of inanimate matter such as the interactions of particles, experiences of living organisms, and subjective conscious experience. The familiar objects of our everyday experience he considers to be constructions based on primary collections of experiences and relationships that endure and have continuity. This view of reality emphasizes the continual flux of change and novelty. In the balance of being and becoming in the world, Whitehead favors becoming.

Is Whitehead an atheist like Marx and Nietzsche? Surprisingly, Whitehead is far from being an atheist. In his book *Religion in the Making*, Whitehead expounds on a view of God that harks back to a mystical picture with a modern twist. Perhaps the novelty he introduces is his way of bringing religious philosophy more into line with modern scientific cosmology.

Whitehead sees God as having two natures, the primordial and the consequent. These natures are apprehensions of God from two points of view, which Whitehead calls abstract and concrete realizations of value. One could describe these two natures as encounters with God's transcendence and immanence. The transcendent encounter experiences God as static, eternal, perfect, and infinite while the immanent God is experienced as finite, fluid, passive, and dependent on the actualized universe. Thus, God is a paradox, at the same time eternal and in flux, the supreme cause and the totality of effects, unity and complexity, passivity and activity, being and becoming, Creator and creature, even the good and the bad. Whitehead seeks a synthesis of these opposites in which there is no separation between God and the creation. In *Religion in the Making*, he calls God Creator-with-the-creatures.

In God's transcendent, perfect aspect, God is unconscious and "deficient in actuality." This might seem contradictory. How could God be perfect and deficient? Imagine that transcendence means pure potentiality, not yet any actuality. Actuality only comes through immanence. Rather than calling transcendent God deficient, one could say that perfection in potentiality is followed by a process called actualization. Actualization falls short of perfection. The world of immanence is limited. What is hinted at here is expressed by the Sufi tradition, "I was a Hidden Treasure and I longed to be known, so I created the world that I might be known."

God's state of perfection and completeness is transcendent, yet desires to know itself in a limited but concrete way. And so, Being begets becoming. Our perception of reality as the flux of experience is the fulfillment of the infinite potential of perfection becoming known, albeit always in limited fashion.

Whitehead's vision is neither theistic (complete separation of God and the world) nor pantheistic (complete identity of God with the world). Rather, reality is seen as an organic unity. He called it "the personality of the cosmic body." In *Process and Reality*, he says, "It is as true to say that God creates the World, as that the World creates God." He goes further, saying this process never reaches completion. He claims, "Either of them, God and the World, is the instrument of novelty for the other."

Whitehead's ideas about God were developed by Charles Hartshorne and John Cobb into a religious form called Process Theology. Some of its themes include:

- God's power is persuasive rather than commanding.
- Everything in the universe has its own self-determination through free will. God does not control this determination but is intimately involved in it.
- God contains the universe but is not the same as the universe. (This idea about reality is called panentheism.)
- God is affected by the changing universe while abstract elements of God such as goodness and wisdom do not change.

The twist that Whitehead has introduced into traditional mystical ideas of theology is the relational interchange between the immanent aspect of God and the creative life of the universe. Rather than having a predetermined plan for the universe, God is engaged in a creative partnership with what God has created from God's own Self. Reality is enriched by this process of actualization, though ultimately God's transcendent aspect is always perfect and complete.

Heidegger

While Whitehead's primary concern was with process and becoming, Martin Heidegger launched a penetrating study of the nature of Being. As with Whitehead, Heidegger doesn't trust rational analysis that abstracts and objectifies signs of reality. He turns instead to direct experience, as Whitehead does, but in a more practical way. He starts with an intuition about the unity of Being. Being is existence and it precedes the duality of subject and object. Being is primordial, it has always been. It doesn't come from anything else. Heidegger is not interested in finding out about Being as an object (or as God), but he wants to understand the meaning of Being for our lives.

As an expression of Being, he calls humans *Dasein*, a German word meaning literally, "being there" or "there being." "There being" implies that our being is there for universal Being. We are an expression, or guardians, of Being. "Being there" suggests that our existence is made meaningful by our practical experience in the world.

Being (with a capital *B*) and being are interdependent; each needs the other. Being is the essence of being. Knowledge of Being is self-revealing. We have a vague, intuitive prior knowledge of Being.

Heidegger believes that one can get closer to the mystery of Being through a process of intense questioning. Living questions are more important than limited answers that may mislead. He felt that the question originally asked by Leibniz, "Why is there something rather than nothing," is "the fundamental question of metaphysics." An insight that follows from this question is that Nothingness or No-thing-ness is not simply emptiness but is rich in possibility. Becoming aware of Nothing can produce anxiety, but it can also reveal something about Being. He sees Nothing as the source of Being. This will become clearer later.

In *Being and Time*, Heidegger investigates Being through an examination of our being. How do we see the world, and how do we function in it? Our involvement in the practical matters of everyday life is an integral part of our beingness. Beyond the practical aspects of our lives, we also function in a social network.

We find ourselves in circumstances and relationships we did not choose. Life propels us continually into new circumstances. These experiences he calls thrownness. Our lives are to some extent defined by thrownness. Against this current, we struggle to discover and fulfill who we are, to fulfill our potential. Besides the constraint of the given or thrownness, we are also conditioned by our social network to be who we are expected to be. There is the additional but related struggle to be our authentic self.

Our conditioned self may be comfortable, but it is inauthentic. We fall into superficial habits to avoid the strain of asserting who we truly are against the tide of social pressure and our thrownness. Typically, we take the easier road and conform. Heidegger is sympathetic to the pressures we are under and the practical role that inauthenticity plays in our everyday lives. He sees the boredom, irritation, and anxiety that arise from the tension of living an inauthentic life as moods that aid us in becoming more aware of the essence of being.

In Heidegger's view, we drift through life conforming to the needs of our conditioned self for the sake of a sense of security and stability. Only by confronting our mortality can we shake this false sense of security. By facing anxiety and bravely accepting responsibility for our life and death, we can begin to live authentically. Facing Nothingness brings true freedom. By means of an existential crisis, we can break free of the enslavement of the conditioned self and decide to make meaning for ourselves in life. Meaning comes by asking ourselves, "What do I truly want in my life?"

When facing Nothingness, one could yield to despair and question why one should do anything in life. What is the point if it all leads to nothing in the end? Heidegger identifies caring as the essential ingredient that makes courageous choices possible. Care is naturally arising. In Buddhism, it is called compassion and is a sign of the awakening of an enlightened consciousness.

For Heidegger, continual awareness of the presence of death, acceptance of its stark meaning, and a conscious choice to find meaning in life is the way to an authentic life. He writes that when we are awake and alive, we are a being-toward-death. Our journey toward Nothingness makes our existence more poignant. It makes us care about what we truly value and move toward it.

> In *Being and Time*, dissatisfied with the results of his discussion of Being, Heidegger stated that words cannot explain the "isness" of Being, which is "intrinsically mysterious and self-concealing," and that attempts to define it or subject it to logical analysis are like "reaching into a void." He concluded that all one could say about it was "Being is Being."[7]

---

7. Michael Watts, *Heidegger: An Essential Guide for Beginners* (London: Hodder & Stoughton, 2001), 215.

Conclusion

We began with the question whether Western philosophy under the growing influence of scientific discovery has turned away from notions of reality dominated by Christian ideas about God and moved toward atheism. Indeed, the influence of Darwin's ideas about evolution in the second half of the nineteenth century can be seen in the explicit atheism of Marx and Nietzsche.

However, the story is not so simple. There seems to be general agreement that rational inquiry into the existence or nature of God is futile. Reality has a hidden dimension that is beyond the capacity of the mind to comprehend. If any knowledge or understanding of it is possible, it must come through other faculties. There seems to be a general rebellion against the idea put forward by scientific materialism that reality is completely determined and mechanical in nature. Spinoza finds an innate goodness in the world and Kant an innate moral compass in humanity. Hegel sees evidence of an historical emergence of self-revealing spirit reflected in an evolution of spiritual values in humanity.

With Marx and Nietzsche, we see a shift from reliance on God or religion to make meaning for us in life to dependence on humanity to provide meaning and to act upon it. This influence of existentialism, calling upon humanity to take responsibility for making reality as it wishes it to be, can be seen in Whitehead's notion of a collaboration between God and humanity in the creative process of unfoldment and in Heidegger's challenge to face death and live life authentically.

At the same time, the idea of a powerful and invisible unity that reveals itself when we make ourselves available persists through the thinking of most of these philosophers. Our common everyday experience of ourselves and the world around us has an apparent reality we take for granted. Science builds on that appearance of reality. Through experiment and rational theory, it arrives at a very different reality far removed from our usual experience. Philosophers examine our everyday experience and probe for its essence and meaning. The philosophers I have reviewed have each added their novel insights about reality. It might be fair to say that Whitehead and Heidegger especially suggest a way of seeing, a process one can follow, to discover the authentic nature of reality, something beyond words and analysis. They claim truth is self-revealing and will disclose itself when one approaches it properly.

Can we say then that Western philosophy has followed the same skeptical path as science and is ready to reject traditional ideas about God? On the contrary, it appears that philosophy has continued to explore the mystical roots behind religious belief in an increasingly generic way, freed of the stories and doctrines of religious tradition, and attempting to understand what motivates us and gives meaning and purpose to our lives.

Part 2

Beyond Negation

Introduction to Part 2

The wonderful thing is that the soul already knows to some extent that there is something behind the veil, the veil of perplexity, that there is something to be sought for in the highest spheres of life, that there is some beauty to be seen, that there is someone to be known who is knowable.
—Hazrat Inayat Khan, *Philosophy, Psychology, Mysticism*

WE HAVE CONSIDERED the influence of modern thinking, especially scientific skepticism, on the question of whether God exists. What we mean by God remains elusive. Science has made spectacular progress in probing the vastness of the macro- and micro-universe, explaining how it works, and unraveling the complexities of life on our planet, the genetic code that shapes it, and the evolutionary process that builds it into ever more elaborate and conscious forms. Yet, much remains a mystery hidden from the reach of science in the inner realms of nature. We have, as Hazrat Inayat Khan refers to, an intuition that something that is knowable lies behind the veil of perplexity. There is another way of knowing that is not rational, that is self-revealing.

Before considering other ways of knowing and their implications for what God might be, several issues from part 1 call for further exploration. In part 1, attention was given to arguments in favor of atheism. Let's examine in more depth some questions that challenge the notion of God: What is consciousness? Is there a Creator? And, why is there evil in the world?

71

4

What Is Consciousness?

Pure Intelligence

MODERN SCIENCE GENERALLY assumes that consciousness is a product of the evolution of the brain. If consciousness arose in its most rudimentary form in the earliest protozoan forms of life about 1.5 billion years ago, it was absent for 90 percent of the 13.8 billion years since the big bang, at least on this particular planet. It is possible that life capable of some form of consciousness developed elsewhere in the universe at an earlier time. However, it seems likely that according to the idea that consciousness is a byproduct of evolution, it was absent for a major part of the life of the universe. I find it difficult to imagine a universe devoid of consciousness for most of its existence, but for others that might seem natural.

Science can only investigate the outer life of nature. Mystics have understood and witnessed for themselves that nature also has an inner life. As scientists are well equipped through training and the use of elaborate technology to study the outer life of nature, so mystics are well equipped to gain insight into the inner life of nature by virtue of their dedication to inner exploration which involves rigorous self-discipline. According to the lore of mystics, consciousness is a property of the inner life of nature, and has always existed in the idealized form of pure intelligence.

What then is the meaning of pure intelligence? Our common notion of intelligence involves a capacity for rational reasoning. The IQ test, although culturally bound, is regarded as a measure of this kind of intelligence. There are other kinds of intelligence. When we watch highly trained athletes, we become aware of physical intelligence, the ability of the body to react more swiftly than the mind. Commentators use the term "good tennis IQ" to describe the expert and instant reaction in a tennis match that produces a precise response to an unexpected challenge. The body seems to have a capacity for instinctive or learned intelligence independent of conscious rumination. Another kind of intelligence has come to light, emotional intelligence, an intelligence not measured by an IQ test. Emotional intelligence is a capacity to recognize emotions in oneself and others and to interact socially in an insightful way. A person with a high degree of rational intelligence is sometimes lacking in emotional intelligence. Then what about wisdom? Wisdom can combine rational and emotional intelligence, surpassing them in its depth, breadth, and humanity. Each of these forms of intelligence is relative, ranging over a scale from low to high.

At the root of each kind of intelligence is something immeasurable. I will call it perfect intelligence. I am assuming it is the source of intelligence in every intelligent creature or object. I also take it to be the source of the feeling of self. If we were to set aside everything in us that is changeable and passing, and disidentify from these things, what would be left? A bare feeling of "I" or self. There would be nothing tangible to associate with that feeling of self. It is that experience of essential self that I would identify with pure intelligence. Although it is difficult to define or describe, the quality of intelligence independent of any intelligent object is easy to recognize. It is the great equalizer because every "I" is linked to something perfect and therefore not comparable from one person to another. In other words, I am suggesting that our sense of self is rooted in universal pure intelligence. The same pure intelligence is presumed to be at the root of every sentient self.

To grasp what pure intelligence means, I need to anticipate what we will explore in part 3. Let's consider a theme of part 3, the mystical notion of reality, in which the condition of unity underlies our common experience of multiplicity or duality. This is the idea that the Real, beyond the understanding of the mind, is a seamless undifferentiated oneness.

Common sense is based on our everyday experience. According to common sense, the world is made up of innumerable separate objects. Each of us seems to be a separate person. We experience a barrier that keeps us isolated and alone, no matter how close we get to others. According to the experience of the mystic, what keeps us isolated and alone is an artificial or conditioned sense of self that has been constructed during our lifetime by the impressions we have taken in. Naturally, we hold on to this sense of self because it allows us to function in everyday life. Heidegger described this artificial sense of self as the inauthentic self.

Many think death will bring about the end of the self. The mystic tries to dislodge the conditioned sense of self before death. The end of the conditioned self doesn't mean the end of a sense of self altogether. Heidegger's approach is to strip away the inauthentic self through the shock of confronting our mortality. The conditioned or inauthentic self is, after all, merely a mental construction. What are we then if we stop clinging to an artificial notion of self? Heidegger reports that by becoming nothing, we discover our authentic self that is free and rich in potential. The mystic reports that when we lose what we have assumed to be our self, we discover the seamless unity that is our inherent nature and links us inseparably with everything and everyone else. Isolation and loneliness disappear. We discover that we are pure intelligence.

We usually think of intelligence on a relative scale. No matter how much intelligence we can imagine a person having, it is possible to imagine a still more intelligent person. We also have the capacity to imagine the perfection of a quality such as intelligence. Perfect intelligence is in its own category. Nothing can be better than perfection. Therefore, perfect intelligence is incomparable.

From the perspective of duality, qualities such as intelligence are always relative. However, one can also imagine a perfect quality that is no longer relative but is absolute. A perfect quality can only be understood from the perspective of unity. From that perspective, it must be one with any other perfected quality. All qualities that are distinct in duality become indistinguishable in unity by their very nature. Thus, mystics understand love, light, and intelligence to be different apprehensions of one thing. This one thing is called spirit.

> We know intelligence as a faculty, but in reality it is spirit itself. No doubt science today may not accept this argument, as the idea of the modern scientist is rather that what we call intelligence is an outcome of matter, that matter has evolved during thousands of years [*sic*] through different aspects and has culminated in the human as a wonderful phenomenon in the form of intelligence. He traces the origin of intelligence to matter. But the mystic holds, as in the past all prophets, saints, and sages have known, that it is spirit which through a gradual action has become denser and has materialized itself into what we call matter or substance. Through this substance it gradually unfolds itself, for it cannot rest in it. It is caught in this denseness, gradually making its way out through a process taking

thousands of years [*sic*], until in the human it develops itself as intelligence.[1]

From a dualistic perspective, spirit can be defined as not matter. We perceive spirit as a vacuum, emptiness, no thing. Yet, from the unitary perspective it is the only existence. Everything derives its existence from spirit or emptiness. Matter is described as a condensation of spirit.

How does spirit as perfect intelligence become consciousness? Consciousness is understood simply as intelligence presented with an object. Without an object to be aware of, intelligence is present but not engaged so there is no consciousness. This definition assumes subjectivity. To become aware of an object, there must be an observing subject. Where does the subject come from?

Mystics conceive the subject as the first thing that emerges as the sleeping all-pervading intelligence wakes up. In the drama of cosmic awakening, the emergence of duality from unity, the first step is awareness of existence as a sea of vibration: both subtle movement or energy and tone in the sense of music. Imagine a throbbing or pulsing that signifies life or vitality in its most abstract form. The first object of awareness is existence itself. There is not yet an awareness of subject even though it is subject that has noticed existence as object. From this first awareness the subject wakes up and realizes "I exist." The second object of awareness is the subject. It is the first stirring of self-awareness.

From a materialist perspective, it appears that subjectivity is a late development in the evolution of matter, and self-awareness is the culmination of subjectivity flowering in human consciousness.

The mystic would say self-awareness was the earliest step in the awakening of consciousness, but that it emerged in the

---

1. Hazrat Inayat Khan, *Philosophy, Psychology, Mysticism*, vol. XI, *The Sufi Message of Hazrat Inayat Khan* (Katwijk: Servire BV, 1964), 59.

realm of emptiness and freedom. The realization "I exist" was an abstract discovery. There was only the bare awareness of "I" and "existence," existence as the sense of vibration or tone and "I" as an intuition of subject without all the associations we attribute to self. The primal self, still ringing with the nature of perfection and all possibility, has to go through the process of condensation or materialization to discover itself in specificity, in richness of detail. Hazrat Inayat Khan describes the paradox of the soul as an apparent individual self and its nature as a universal or primal self.

> It is as great a mistake not to know where our soul is, as it is to believe that we have no soul at all. The soul is like a piece of cloth round which a line is drawn, confining a part of it, and making it distinct from the rest of the cloth. The best simile is this: if we stand with a small lantern before a curtain, the light of the lantern will be reflected on the curtain, and will form a round patch. So the impressions of the mind and body are reflected upon the soul, but when the mind is dispersed, no impression will remain upon the soul, nothing will separate it from the whole of the consciousness.[2]

The picture I have described of universal intelligence and consciousness has sometimes been called panpsychism. It is an ancient philosophy traced back to the Greeks and further developed by the Neoplatonists and modern philosophers like Schopenhauer, Spinoza, William James, Whitehead, and Bertrand Russell. Contemporary philosophers are showing renewed interest in panpsychism.

While the ideas of universal consciousness and soul reported by the mystics resemble conceptual ideas of panpsychism, the mystical perspective can never be reduced to a

2. Hazrat Inayat Khan, "Metaphysics III," *The Supplementary Papers* (privately published).

conceptual theory. There is an inherent mystery in these insights that defies the capabilities of the human mind. The ideas presented here are very limited approximations of the experience of mystics, experiences that cannot be conveyed in words or thoughts.

How to Define Consciousness

One of the reasons scientists find consciousness difficult to investigate is that it is problematic to define. Philosopher David Chalmers suggested dividing the investigation of consciousness into two parts. The easy problem for science is to trace how sensations are transmitted to the brain and what the brain does with them. This is the study of neural processes in the brain associated with perception. He describes the hard problem of consciousness research this way:

> The hard problem, in contrast, is the question of how physical processes in the brain give rise to subjective experience. This puzzle involves the inner aspect of thought and perception: the way things feel for the subject.[3]

The lack of a clear definition of consciousness has also hampered research on animal consciousness. Although many experiments have documented aspects of conscious behavior in animals that parallel human behavior—such as problem solving to gain a reward and recognition in a mirror of marks made on the animal that cannot otherwise be seen—scientists are not able to make a definitive scientific statement about whether animals are conscious. Nonetheless, in 2012 a gathering of prominent neuroscientists made

---

3. David Chalmers, "The Puzzle of Conscious Experience," *Scientific American* 273, no. 6 (December 1995): 2.

the Cambridge Declaration on Consciousness that included this summary:

> We decided to reach a consensus and make a statement directed to the public that is not scientific. It's obvious to everyone in this room that animals have consciousness, but it is not obvious to the rest of the world. It is not obvious to the rest of the Western world or the Far East. It is not obvious to the society.[4]

Convergent evidence indicates that nonhuman animals have the neuroanatomical, neurochemical, and neurophysiological substrates of conscious states along with the capacity to exhibit intentional behaviors. Consequently, the weight of evidence indicates that humans are not unique in possessing the neurological substrates that generate consciousness. Nonhuman animals, including all mammals and birds, and many other creatures, including octopuses, also possess these neurological substrates.[5]

It is much harder for science to get at the inner experience of consciousness.

A simple definition of consciousness is intelligence presented with an object. When intelligence becomes aware of something, it becomes conscious. By this definition, certainly, animals are conscious. They are aware of their surroundings and respond to them appropriately. This behavior is not limited to more complex organisms. The biologist Brian Ford describes how testate amoebae construct shells to live in from grains of sand gathered from silt.[6] The amoebae are selective about what materials they use. Different species of amoebae choose different materials. They are able to distinguish in the

---

4. "Consciousness," Wikipedia, https://en.wikipedia.org/wiki/Consciousness.

5. "Cambridge Declaration on Consciousness," fcmconference.org/img/CambridgeDeclarationOnConsciousness.pdf, 2012.

6. Brian Ford, *Biologist* 53, no. 4 (August 2006): 222.

silt the kind of material they prefer, select it out, and build their shells from it. By the criterion of awareness, they are surely conscious.

Are plants conscious? The book and film *The Secret Life of Plants* seemed to establish a case for plant consciousness. Scientists subsequently criticized the evidence presented in the book as false or unsupported by independent verification. However, the idea has been resurrected by serious plant biologists in a new field called plant neurobiology. In 2013, Michael Pollan reported on progress in this field in the *New Yorker*.[7] He points out that plant activity operates on a much slower timescale than we are used to. Time-lapse photography confirms the sensitive responsiveness of plants to their environment. An especially striking time-lapse video shows two green-bean runners on either side of a pole. As the runners grow, they both weave around, moving toward the pole they somehow detect. One of the plants reaches the pole first and begins to wrap its tendril around it. The other runner seems to recognize it has lost the race. It weaves to one side of the pole as though searching for something else for support. Finding nothing, it gradually retreats and wilts. From appearances, the runners somehow are aware of the presence of the pole, and the runner that lost the race appears to be aware of the winner.[8] From the simple definition of consciousness, because the runners are aware, they are conscious.

Scientists who study animals look for neurological processes related to human brain structure as evidence that animals are capable of consciousness, as the Cambridge Declaration on Consciousness shows. From the perspective of the inner life of nature, behavior might be a better indicator of conscious awareness. If intelligence is universal, it may find myr-

7. Michael Pollan, "The Intelligent Plant," *New Yorker*, December 23 and 30, 2013.

8. "Plant Neurobiology, Commentary, the *New Yorker*," July 2014, YouTube, www.youtube.com/watch?v=MPql1VHbYl4.

iad ways to become aware of other objects once it settles into the functioning of a self or observer. In the most rudimentary sense, the reactions of charged particles encountering each other, for instance, could be considered a form of awareness. Ordinarily, we think of awareness as calculating intelligence. Awareness implies having a choice of how to respond. It is not automatic. Of course, we have reflexes that are automatic. Our body is aware of its environment and can respond without mental awareness by way of the body's physical intelligence. Reflexes are routed through neural circuits that only go as far as the spinal cord. We could say that the body is conscious without using the apparatus of the brain. Automatic reactions become mentally conscious after the fact and autonomic reactions such as those that control heartbeat and breathing can elude our ordinary state of consciousness.

Inner knowledge from the experience of mystics indicates that intelligence has always been present. It is always seeking better instruments to accommodate it. In the simplest forms of matter, intelligence gains awareness through the fixed reactions captured in the laws of physics. The life of elementary particles is limited to the interactions that occur because of their "awareness" of each other through the elementary forces of gravitation, electromagnetism, and weak and strong nuclear forces. In this limited sense, they are conscious, though much less so than our ordinary sense of consciousness.

A more subtle conception of consciousness is conveyed by the metaphor of a mirror. An object placed before a mirror is reflected in the mirror. When the object is removed, the mirror reverts to blankness, though it still has its capacity to reflect. Consciousness deprived of an object still has a holding capacity. Is a person in an isolation chamber with no object or impression to take into consciousness then unconscious? The holding capacity is still there. One can be alert and aware in an isolation chamber when the field of consciousness is empty of stimuli. Consciousness can be alert with attention at the ready, with its holding capacity open, when there is no impression to take in. At such a time, there could be plenty of stimulus from the inner life. Thoughts, imaginations, and feelings don't require external prompting. Ultimately, the final object of attention before becoming unconscious is awareness itself. Consciousness can be aware of being aware, conscious of the capacity to perceive and understand.

The notion of consciousness as a capacity goes back to the idea of pure intelligence. When intelligence is confronted by an object and becomes consciousness, it is still perfect intelligence, its original condition. Consciousness then, as pure intelligence, is the undifferentiated invisible oneness underlying all appearances, which I have called spirit.

> For an instance, a mirror with a reflection is not only a mirror, but it is a mirror with reflection. There is something already reflected in it. That means it is occupied, it is not empty. When a person says "consciousness," he cannot think of the original condition. He thinks only of the consciousness which is conscious of something. As soon as you distinguish between the consciousness and what it is conscious of, you separate them, you see them as two things, as you separate the mirror from what is reflected in it.[9]

According to this view of things, our ordinary experience of consciousness, so essential to our experience of being a person, is in its underlying condition a direct apprehension of spirit, an invisible universal essence. Science may be able to determine how consciousness works in the brain, what Chalmers posited as the "easy" problem of consciousness research, but it remains stumped by the hard problem, because

---

9. Hazrat Inayat Khan, *Complete Works, Original Texts: Lectures on Sufism*, 1926 I (New Lebanon, NY: Omega Publications, 2010), 219.

spirit can never be measured by material means. There is no way to measure something that is perfect and unlimited or infinite.

A Measure of Consciousness

While consciousness as the mirror cannot be measured, we can measure what is held in the mirror. In other words, the capacity of the instrument that is holding consciousness can be measured. We are familiar with limited forms of consciousness such as confusion, drowsiness, dementia, and coma. It is medically important to be able to determine whether a person in an extended state of coma is conscious. Consciousness research is seeking a method for measuring degrees of consciousness in animals such as primates, crows, parrots, octopuses, and even some insects.

Traditionally, consciousness has been inferred in scientific studies by observing behavior, subjects' reports, or the measurement of neuronal correlates (for example, through brain imaging including EEGs). Tononi and Koch have combined these measures in what they call Integrated Information Theory (IIT).[10] Unlike most scientists, they assume consciousness to be intrinsic rather than emergent through brain evolution. They take their cues from their understanding of the experience of consciousness. To determine whether a human subject is conscious, they look at all the information available from neuronal correlates, the measures of brain activity. They then look for a maximum of the integrated information, the collected neuronal measures of brain activity, sufficient to describe a state of awareness based on observed behavior as well as subjects' reports. In other words, they

10. Giulio Tononi and Christof Koch, "Consciousness: Here, There and Everywhere?," Philosophical Transactions of the Royal Society B 370, May 19, 2015, https://doi.org/10.1098/rstb.2014.0167.

calibrate their measures based on the reports of subjects who are able to indicate their awareness, then apply the results to subjects who are not.

Tononi and Koch set out basic assumptions about consciousness from self-observation. According to their axioms, consciousness is inherent, structured, coherent, integrated, and distinct. Inherent means that it is present as a fundamental property of nature. From self-reflection consciousness is experienced as structured because it recognizes objects and their relationships and as coherent because it differentiates features of objects in a systematic way. Consciousness is seen as integrated because we perceive in wholes and parts; perceived reality hangs together and makes sense. Consciousness is distinct rather than fuzzy because we incorporate all the details we observe into a coherent whole.

From this axiomatic picture of conscious experience, the authors make a set of assumptions (called postulates) about the neuronal mechanisms that support consciousness. If consciousness exists intrinsically, the supporting brain structure has developed in response to intrinsic consciousness rather than being the source of consciousness. The activity or inactivity of the neuronal mechanisms also indicate how much consciousness is present.

The structure and coherence of an experience of consciousness depend on how the component parts of the mental mechanism work together. When the parts function as a whole and coherently, consciousness is full. A quantitative measure of awareness can be inferred from how the various neuronal measures are correlated and thereby interdependent, and how much they are activated. Ideally the quality and quantity of a conscious experience could be fully captured if all the interacting physical mechanisms were known and their state of engagement and interaction could be measured.

Tononi and Koch also discuss how IIT may be related to ideas of panpsychism, the notion that reality is composed of one phenomenon underlying the multiplicity of appearances. By considering consciousness as an intrinsic attribute in nature, IIT suggests a principle of unity. It stops short of attributing consciousness to everything inanimate as well as animate. It does, however, concede the mystery of consciousness, foregoing the materialist claim that consciousness can be explained as an outcome of evolution or an epiphenomenon.

From the mystical point of view, IIT recognizes that consciousness is intrinsic and offers a quantifiable way to measure limited consciousness. However, its method of detecting consciousness is limited to the presence of measurable neuronal mechanisms. Plants, for example, do not have the neuronal mechanisms found in animals, yet there may be evidence of plant consciousness. As we have noted, amoebae also do not have incipient brains, yet they show signs of awareness.

If consciousness arises in the inner life of nature, then IIT may offer an example of how scientific and mystical insight could meet at the boundary between inner and outer perspectives. With consciousness on one side and measurement of neuronal correlates on the other, there may be a meeting place where collaboration could happen. This approach would require sobriety from both scientists and mystics with each remaining open to the other and surrendering claims of preeminence.

While IIT offers an admirable advance for science in studying the easy problem of consciousness, the difficulties science has in tackling the hard problem remain.

Cosmic Idealism

David Chalmers, after examining many forms of idealism, finds the most promising philosophically to be cosmic idealism. He defines cosmic idealism as "the thesis that all concrete facts are grounded in facts about the mental states of a single cosmic entity, such as the universe as a whole or perhaps a god." It may be inevitable that a philosopher would give privileged status to the mind, since it is the realm of philosophical inquiry.

> When I was in graduate school, I recall hearing "One starts as a materialist, then one becomes a dualist, then a panpsychist, and one ends up as an idealist." I don't know where this comes from, but I think the idea was something like this. First, one is impressed by the successes of science, endorsing materialism about everything and so about the mind. Second, one is moved by [the] problem of consciousness to see a gap between physics and consciousness, thereby endorsing dualism, where both matter and consciousness are fundamental. Third, one is moved by the inscrutability of matter to realize that science reveals at most the structure of matter and not its underlying nature, and to speculate that this nature may involve consciousness, thereby endorsing panpsychism. Fourth, one comes to think that there is little reason to believe in anything beyond consciousness and that the physical world is wholly constituted by consciousness, thereby endorsing idealism.[11]

Chalmers describes the progression of thinking about reality from the perspective of an isolated self, questioning the nature of its experience and whether experience has any

11. David Chalmers, "Idealism and the Mind-Body Problem," in *The Routledge Handbook of Panpsychism*, ed. William Seager (New York: Routledge, 2021), 353.

objective validity. As long as one is encapsulated in the perspective of an individual separate witness, precision in one's observations inevitably leads back to the observing mind, the locus of experience. Thus, recognizing the apparent existence of a vast cosmos, one can extrapolate from the nexus of experience in the mind to a cosmic or universal mind, of which the human mind, according to the mystics, is somehow an artifact.

Philosophically, the idea of cosmic idealism comes closest to the mystical point of view about consciousness. However, as mentioned earlier, the mystical perspective on reality cannot be reduced to a conceptual "ism."

For cosmic idealism as a philosophy, Chalmers poses three challenges: the constitution problem, the relationality problem, and the austerity problem.

The constitution problem highlights the difficulty of explaining how a cosmic mind, if it exists, gives rise to the individual mind of human experience. What is the connection between cosmic mind and human mind? What answer does the mystical perspective as I have described it offer to this problem?

The cosmic mind experiences pure intelligence. As that intelligence is threaded through the consciousness of human individuals, it gains awareness of its own nature through experience. It moves from the abstract realm of the cosmic mind to the concrete expression of the human mind. From the mystical point of view, the essence of individual experience is reported back to the centralized intelligence to be shared with all subsequent individuals as the nectar harvested from the complexity of manifested life. Cosmic experience, then, is the amalgam of the essence of individual experience of innumerable witnesses. Human experience both benefits from and adds to this inheritance through each individual's unique experience.

Another response to the constitution problem is that the human individual inherits from the cosmic mind various capacities that have become articulated in the instrument of the body, mind, and heart. The capacities of the senses such as seeing and hearing, abstract in the cosmic mind, have developed over vast stretches of time into the mechanisms of eyes and ears. Other inherited capacities have developed into our rationality or mathematical sense. In the experience of cosmic mind, these capacities—such as responsiveness to vibration or light—are archetypal. In human experience, these abstract capacities take on form and function.

Cosmic idealism regards only mental states as real. The relationality problem challenges idealism by claiming that there are abstract objects that are not mental states grounded in experience. For example, an archetype, such as blueness, is not experiential. We experience a blue color, an exemplar of an archetype. Although we can grasp the archetype of blueness, we don't experience it directly. Thus we can't call an archetype a mental state. The cosmic mind, prior to manifestation, encounters only abstractions such as archetypes. But then how can it be mind only if abstract objects are not mental states? If we don't insist on mind as fundamental but rather take pure intelligence as the single subject, the cosmic intelligence rather than the cosmic mind, the problem goes away because the experience of cosmic consciousness is the realm of archetypes. The mystic claims that it is possible to have an experience of an archetype, a non-ordinary mental state.

The austerity problem arises because on a cosmic scale, experience seems to be essentially the simple interactions of particles described by the laws of physics. Cosmic idealism is called austere because it is governed by austere laws as compared with the complex behaviors of living and thinking beings. The laws of physics may be the most rudimentary form of consciousness, as the four basic forces of nature are responsible for a form of "awareness" among elementary particles. Biological evolution proceeds through the formation of more complex forms out of simpler ones.

Cosmic intelligence needn't be austere. Since it contains all possibilities, one could say that what has evolved on earth over billions of years, although complex to the understanding of our minds, is austere in comparison to the unlimited possibilities still undisclosed in the imagination of perfect intelligence. The problem seems to be reversed. Rather than being austere, cosmic idealism is an embarrassment of riches.

It is not intelligence that is austere but the instruments through which intelligence must function that have evolved from austerity to the present state of complexity. There is no problem of austerity from the mystical perspective. Pure intelligence does not change over time. It is always the same in its perfection. The complexity of human behavior and experience derives from the profusion of perfection. Science has shown how the richness of experience has become more evident as the instruments of consciousness have evolved through natural selection.

The Visibility Problem

Science deals with measurable phenomena. Measurable information comes through our senses and through instruments that enhance our perceptual capabilities. What is invisible to our sensorium or instruments is relegated to the realm of speculation or dismissed as unreliable and subjective. Pure intelligence is invisible to our consensus reality. We cannot see it because it is at the center of our perceptual apparatus. We see all things around us with our eyes, but we cannot see our eyes without some sort of mirror. Pure intelligence is what we are looking out of, so to speak. We cannot see our selfhood, what makes us feel like a self, looking out.

The things at the root of consciousness—self, pure intelligence, and soul—are invisible.

> The external self, the mind and body have formed the individual self. The mind sees the body and the soul sees the body and the mind. The body cannot see the mind, neither the body nor the mind is able to see the soul. The only possibility that remains is for the soul to see itself. But the soul cannot see itself without a mirror, just as the eyes cannot see themselves without a mirror. Our soul has always looked outward. That is why the eyes are outward, the nose is outward. It is our mind and our body that attract our soul outward.[12]

Mystics train themselves to turn the senses inward. In the mirror of the inner life, the soul perceives itself. What appeared to be an individual self, separate from others, is directly understood as a universal Self, functioning in a particular body and mind, with a personality of innate tendencies and qualities that have been influenced by the impressions of life's experiences. At first, the mystic might have the feeling of witnessing its former identification as a limited self. With a broadened perspective, the universal Self can inhabit the personality and invest it with a deeper faith in the unlimited source from which it draws. A stream of consciousness that was limited by the defensive shell of an insecure individual can now run free providing a bounty of creativity and inspiration.

Insatiable curiosity drives the mind to seek satisfaction in understanding how things work, their interrelationships, and the intricacy of nature and thought. The intellect is gratified by ever greater unraveling of the mysteries of the world around us. Another kind of satisfaction arises from appreciation of the exquisite beauty of nature and the achievements of artistic creativity. There is a satisfaction of the heart when

12. Hazrat Inayat Khan, "Metaphysics III," *The Supplementary Papers*.

it opens to experience love in all its forms. And a spiritual fulfillment develops from deep inner experiences that feel sacred and establish firm faith.

Philosophers note that we are able to discern the properties of objects but not their essence, what Kant called the thing-in-itself. What is it that gives us a feeling of satisfaction from an experience? When we are gratified by a discovery, moved by beauty, touched by love, or uplifted by a deep realization something has been accomplished, a purpose has been fulfilled. It is a purpose of the whole universe, of the universal intelligence acting through us. We are each a unique door of discovery through which the primal Self is coming to know itself. The consciousness of which we are aware is the way we perceive what is actually a universal probing consciousness that is in us and around us, wherever we turn.

Conclusion

When we examine consciousness in the light of the discoveries of mystics, we come to a different understanding than the idea of science that consciousness is a byproduct of evolution. I have suggested that nature has both an outer and an inner life. Science has advanced our knowledge of the outer material life to such a degree that it now proposes to discover a theory of everything encompassing all physical aspects of the universe. Nothing is to be excluded from its compass including consciousness. We have seen that some scientists believe consciousness cannot be explained from material causes such as mass or electric charge but must be taken as intrinsic. Nonetheless, this kind of intrinsic consciousness is considered to be part of the outer life of the world, a basic property of matter.

While a theory of everything would be incomplete without an appreciation of the nature of consciousness, the ideas presented in this chapter do not fit neatly into a theory of any kind. Ideas have been suggested to point toward an elusive reality ultimately inaccessible to the mind or theory itself. According to mystics, the reality alluded to here is only accessible to direct experience through cultivation of inner attention. Nevertheless, I am hopeful that the discoveries of scientists and the insights of mystics can lead to a fuller understanding of our lives and the nature of the universe.

5

Is There a Creator?

No Creator

ORGANISMS HAVE SUCH intricate and complicated designs that it would be natural to attribute them to a brilliant artist and technician. It took the genius of Charles Darwin to recognize that a simple mechanism operating over an extensive period of time can explain what appears to be the operation of a supernatural intelligence. Darwin observed small differences in the beaks of finches on the Galapagos Islands and noted that each kind of beak suited the microenvironment in which he found them. Assuming that at each birth of an organism, small changes can happen by chance, Darwin reasoned that the best changes give the particular organism a survival advantage over others while changes that confer no advantage or are a handicap die out over time. Thus, small changes eventually promote fitness and adaptation to the environment. Familiar with paleontology's discoveries in relation to the fossil record, Darwin realized that evolution takes place over extensive periods of time. Thus, even if minor changes create small advantages that dominate fellow organisms only after many generations or geological periods of time, these small changes can explain a continual evolution of species with all of their complex designs.

Neo-Darwinists have found a mechanism that explains how Darwin's small changes continually occur. DNA is the carrier of heredity for all living organisms. The human body continually replicates DNA in early development and throughout the life span. Replication involves copying three billion nucleotide pairs, which make up the DNA strands. Because bonds between atoms in nucleotide molecules are unstable, occasionally there are mistakes in copied nucleotides. Repair enzymes correct most of these mistakes. A few mutations go through uncorrected and become permanent and can be passed down to future generations.

Neo-Darwinists seek explanations for traits in organisms based not only on their fitness for survival but also on the likelihood they will be transmitted through reproduction. For example, the elaborate plumage of certain types of male birds presumably makes them more attractive to females, though it might not improve their adaptation to the local environment. The term natural selection is therefore preferred over survival of the fittest.

The inevitability of Darwin's explanation of design in nature was the clincher for Dawkins in adopting atheism. Dawkins was presumably so impressed with the apparent role of intelligence in nature's designs that he would have attributed them to a Creator if Darwin's theory of evolution hadn't been so convincing.

Similarly, the cosmologist Stephen Hawking conceded that if no explanation for the origin of the universe could be found through natural law, one would have to accept that it was the work of a Creator. He proposed two ways in which the origin of the universe could be explained without a Creator. One uses the metaphor of the earth's geographic grid. If one moves north above the equator to increasingly higher latitudes, the circle of latitude gets smaller and smaller. When one reaches the North Pole, the latitude circle shrinks to a point and every direction from there is south. One can go no further north. By analogy, if one moves across the curved space-time of the universe toward earlier and earlier times, the dimension of space-time gets increasingly small. When one reaches the singularity 13.8 billion years ago, perhaps space-time becomes so tightly curved that one reaches a pole of time. Attempting to go further only leads to later times. One cannot go to an earlier time from that place.

Hawking's other proposal attempts to explain why the basic physical constants such as the charge of an electron and the ratio of electron and proton masses are so finely tuned that if changed by a very small amount, living organisms would not have been possible. His idea is based on the use of a calculating tool in quantum mechanics called a Feynman diagram. This diagram represents the interaction of elementary particles. Besides the straightforward interaction one would expect from two objects colliding, there are many interactions that one would consider bizarre from ordinary experience with everyday objects but are still possible in the strange quantum world. Feynman concluded that every imaginable interaction must be counted to predict the overall probability of an interaction. Although each of the more unusual interactions makes a small contribution to the total probability, when the probabilities of these extra types of interaction are included in the overall predicted probability, the result agrees with experiments with extreme accuracy to many decimal places.

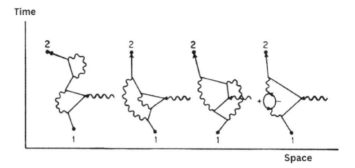

Time

Space

Figure 5. Feynman diagram. A straight line represents the path of an electron, a wiggly line the path of a photon. Each diagram represents a possible interaction of electron 1 encountering a photon moving horizontally from right to left and leaving as electron 2.
Image from Richard Feynman, QED: *The Strange Theory of Light and Matter* (Princeton, NJ: Princeton University Press, 2006), 117.

Hawking applies this idea from quantum mechanics to a collection of universes, called a multiverse. The existence of a multiverse is a further speculation that has some plausible justification. If our universe is one of many universes, then by analogy with the quantum mechanical reality in which all possible variations of two particle interactions contribute to the outcome of an encounter, perhaps the different universes have all imaginable variations in the basic constants of physics. Our universe happens to be where the constants are just right to support living organisms as we know them. Rather than explain anything, this proposal reflects the possibility that nature simply acts as it does; namely, when nature has the opportunity to take many routes, it doesn't favor any particular one but gives each its due.

If there is no need to believe in a Creator to explain the miracle of the creation, something is lost besides a challenge to specific religious beliefs. In the Bible it says that God created the heavens and earth in seven days: "Now God saw all that he had made, and here: it was exceedingly good!"[1]

If there is no Creator and the universe has come about by mechanical means without any design or intent, and if organic life has come about also in a mechanical way through random mutations shaped by environmental constraints, again without design or purpose, then is the world good? Are we not then at the mercy of an uncaring, random, heartless mechanism of a world? Are our lives meaningless and bereft of purpose?

Intelligent Design

Since the time of Darwin, there have been numerous attempts to criticize the theory of natural selection with the intention of showing that some sort of supernatural intervention is still needed to explain the appearance of intelligent design in nature. These efforts have in recent times been referred to as theories of intelligent design.

A major argument of intelligent design is that Darwinian evolution cannot explain irreducible complexity. Something is said to be irreducibly complex if it is made up of many critical parts that are themselves complex and would require presumably separate paths of evolution. How could a body's organ have developed its separate parts without some anticipation of what was needed to complete it? In other words, an intentional design is required rather than a random accumulation of features. An example that is often given is the eye.

Scientists have been able to show that eyes indeed can develop in a gradual way through small steps. The fossil record is not very helpful because soft tissue is not preserved. However, eyes in some form exist in most animals. By studying the

1. Genesis 1:31, *The Schocken Bible*, vol. 1, *The Five Books of Moses*, trans. Everett Fox (New York: Schocken Books, 1983).

changing nature of eyes in modern animals as they become more complex, it is possible to make a plausible explanation for how the various parts of the eye could have developed alongside each other through the process of natural selection.

Other examples of irreducible complexity as suggested by proponents of intelligent design such as blood clotting, the immune system, and flagellum (the tiny motors that propel some bacteria) have all been reasonably explained by scientists as processes of gradual development. The arguments of intelligent design have been seriously considered by scientists but are generally viewed by them as pseudoscience.

Genetics and Embryology

The discovery of DNA as a universal carrier of heredity in animals and plants led to the expectation that mapping the genomes of species would reveal their blueprints. What was revealed instead was a surprise. Human and chimpanzee genomes differ by only 1.5 percent. Mouse genomes also contain 90 percent of the human genome. Not only is DNA quite similar between notably different organisms, the number of genes responsible for forming the protein building blocks of organisms is also much smaller than expected. For humans, apes, and mice, this number is about 35,000. There are 3.5 billion nucleotides or coding elements in DNA. About 2 percent of the human genome's DNA is used for the coding that builds proteins. The remaining 98 percent was once called junk DNA, when it was thought that it had no role to play in the shaping and functioning of an organism. More recent research has shown that the noncoding portions of DNA play many complicated roles that have biological implications.

The idea that there is a linear relationship between genes and resulting traits in organisms has given rise to an industry called genetic modification. By modifying specific genes in plants, biotech companies produce genetically modified organism (GMO) products purported to have specific traits such as resistance to pests. Current research is attempting to apply the same principles to human gene modification to mitigate vulnerability to specific diseases. The underlying idea is called genetic determinism.

The simplified process of protein production by genes involves a few steps. A molecule called messenger ribonucleic acid (mRNA), which is present in all living things, copies the instructions in the gene from its location on the DNA chain in a cell nucleus. Next, the messenger RNA moves into the cytoplasm of the cell and binds to a ribosome, a molecular complex based on another form of RNA. The ribosome reads the code in the copied gene and makes amino acids according to the coded instructions with the help of what is called transfer RNA (tRNA). The ribosome also links the amino acids to form the desired protein. Finally, the proteins must be folded into complex shapes. Proteins are the building blocks of all the structures in the body. For example, they function as enzymes, hormones, and collagen (bones and skin).

This is an oversimplified picture of what happens. There are several reasons why there is often not a linear relationship between genes and traits. For example, genes can be modified in many ways by noncoding genes before making proteins. They can also be modified in response to environmental conditions. Proteins resulting from the same coding may fold in different ways leading to different traits. Traits can result from the influence of a combination of genes. Genes also can be inhibited or activated before they generate proteins. Any correspondence between gene and trait can vary.

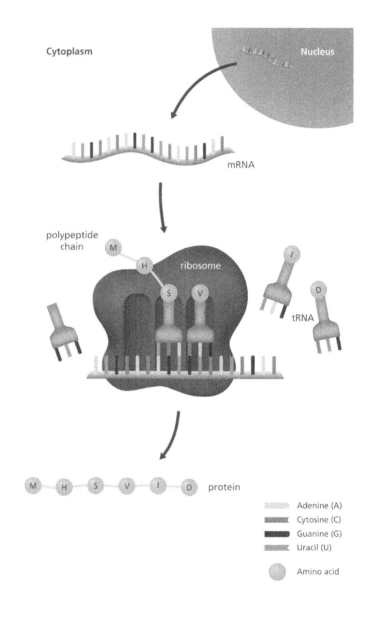

Figure 6. Production of proteins from DNA. Illustration credit Laura Olivares Boldú / Wellcome Connecting Science, via yourgenome.org.

Are there other factors involved in the shaping and forming of organisms besides protein production controlled by genes? In contrast to geneticists, embryologists have their own point of view. Embryology is the study of the formation of organisms starting with the joining of the female egg cell and male sperm cell. For humans, a two-week germinal stage is followed by a six-week embryonic stage of development, after which the embryo is called a fetus.

The pioneering embryologist Erich Blechschmidt was the first to study in detail the rapid development of the human embryo. His laboratory produced sixty-four three-dimensional models of embryonic stages. He wrote several books detailing the complex process of embryo development. He concluded that the morphology of the developing organism is shaped largely by gravitational and thermodynamic influences.

Blechschmidt called the development of the embryo a biodynamic process. As the embryo expands by cell mitosis, it is constrained by the uterine space it fills, by the flow of nutrients, and the expelling of waste. At every moment, the embryo must function as a whole organism, constantly adapting to new conditions and crises. Watching this process unfold moment by moment makes it clear it is a living process, not the mechanical assembly of a machine. Gene activity provides the protein materials for the assembly of all the necessary parts. The assembly itself is responsive, sensitive, and adaptive. The availability of proteins cannot explain the resourcefulness of the embryo in its tortuous journey toward the emergence of a living person. Stephen Talbott, a senior researcher at the Nature Institute and a commentator on biological evolution, calls this kind of resourcefulness *teleological*, an inherently goal-directed behavior.

All biological activity, even at the molecular level, can be characterized as purposive and goal-directed. As a cell grows and divides, it marshals its molecular and structural resources with a remarkably skillful "wisdom." It also demonstrates a well-directed, "willful" persistence in adjusting to disturbances. Everything leads toward fulfillment of the organism's evident "purposes."[2]

Noting the confusion this term might suggest, Talbott distinguishes between purposive behavior that is familiar to us, our conscious planning to achieve a goal, and what he means by teleology, "giving expression to the wholeness of (the organism's) own nature." It is as though the embryo has a built in urge to express itself as a whole and complete organism. This drive can be seen in the embryo's adaptive behavior as it encounters crises at each step along the way.

Author and anthropologist Richard Grossinger writes passionately about the mysteries of life. Commenting on Blechschmidt's biodynamic picture of the emerging human form, he writes:

What ignites and enforces organized activity? What keeps it assembling intricate superstructures, one over another? What is the kernel at the center of the coordination of molecular events leading to cell cohesion and tissue function? What is the partner of hereditary biodynamics? What departs with the last breath? If it is not a spirit choosing an organic-carbon method of incarnation and assembling a molecular vehicle around itself, inhabiting it from within at every vacuole and interstice, then it does one hell of an impression of it.[3]

2. Stephen L. Talbott, "Evolution and the Purposes of Life," *New Atlantis*, no. 51 (Winter 2017): 63–91.

3. Richard Grossinger, *Embryos, Galaxies, and Sentient Beings* (Berkeley, CA: North Atlantic Books, 2003), 393.

Taking up Talbott's idea of teleology, I would use different words to refer to the inherent drive to find expression in fullness. I would use the words desire and will. It seems that the neo-Darwinists have overlooked something fundamental to the idea of natural selection. The desire to live is so universal in living things that it is easy to take for granted. Single-celled organisms seek to escape from their predators. Where does that desire come from? How does one go from complex far-from-equilibrium molecular reactions that create order from chaos and suggest possible precursors for primitive organisms, to simple cells that try to stay alive?

Those molecules that have somehow stumbled on the survival reaction will survive, and those that haven't will die out relatively quickly. Can genetics explain how a desire to live could arise by accident? Without this desire, how can natural selection function? The idea that there is some inherent desire to live and, as Talbott writes, a desire to express the wholeness of the organism's nature, appear to be significant additions to the genetic formulation of evolution. Does this imply that there is a supernatural power, a Creator, working behind the scenes? Yes and no.

A Mystical View of Creation

Much of the difficulty in the question of whether a supernatural Creator exists arises from our way of thinking and speaking. Our understanding is based on dualistic thinking. We experience ourselves as separate individuals. When we speak of a supernatural Creator, many of us naturally think of a separate Being that is outside the world it creates. Mystics have a different experience. They understand reality as a unified oneness (this will be explored in greater depth in part 3). Therefore, a Creator cannot be separate from nature. Rather, nature is an expression of the Creator. The

Creator can be found in every object in the creation from elementary particles to stars, galaxies, planets, rocks, plants, animals, and humans. The Sufi mystic Hazrat Inayat Khan puts it this way:

> Man is not made by God as the wood is cut by the carpenter; for the carpenter and the wood are different, while God and man are the same. Man is made of the same substance of God; man is in God, and all that is in God, is in man.[4]

Talbott's observation that there seems to be an inherent drive in organisms to express their wholeness tallies with a mystical insight. The mystic understands this drive as the Creator or essential spirit working its way through dense matter seeking to find increasingly better ways to express and to come to know itself. Hazrat Inayat Khan notes this mystical vision of evolution as a Sufi tradition:

> There is a saying of the Sufis that "God slept in the rock, God dreamed in the tree, God became self-conscious in the animal, but God sought Himself and recognized Himself in man."[5]

It is difficult to free oneself from dualistic thinking. When God is used in these quotes, no doubt despite the meaning intended, one tends to think of God as a separate supernatural being. If, on the other hand, we say that God is not supernatural but the essential spirit animating nature, we limit God to whatever we can learn of nature. Unity means everything, not only everything that has materialized but also

4. Hazrat Inayat Khan, *Complete Works, Original Texts: Sayings*, part II (London: East-West Publications, 1990), 217.

5. Hazrat Inayat Khan, "The Expansion of Consciousness," in *Healing; Mental Purification; The Mind World*, vol. IV, *The Sufi Message of Hazrat Inayat Khan* (Surrey, UK: Servire Publishing Co., 1961), 231.

every possibility that has yet to be realized. Rather than pin it down that the Creator is natural or supernatural, we could say that nature is the outer life of the Creator and spirit is the Creator's inner life. To avoid returning to dualism, we can say that the outer and inner lives are two aspects of one thing. One merges into the other. There is no definite boundary between them.

How is this different from intelligent design? Following Talbott's lead, we could say that there appears to be an inherent desire in organisms to express fully their nature. Could the Creator be a living essence driven by the desire to experience and know itself, not only in organic things but even in every material object, electrons, atoms, molecules, and rocks? Is this the nature of universal consciousness that rests on the foundation of pure intelligence? One could say that the Creator is a living conscious impulse and the whole creation is an outcome of this impulse.

In the Bible, "God said, Let there be light! And there was light" (Genesis 1:3). In the Qur'an, we have, "Surely His Command, when He wills a thing, is only to say to it: 'Be!' And it is!" (36:82). What does this say about creation? We experience our own creativity as something that comes to us spontaneously. It may come after a period of intense concentration or persevering desire. Scientists who have struggled to understand how nature works have received sudden visions in their imaginations or in their dreams. Artists deeply absorbed in their craft have created masterworks and afterward asked themselves, "Where did that come from?" There appears to be a source of novelty that comes when the spirit is moved. It is a combination of desire and imagination. A mystic would say love and intelligence balance each other. Love is motivated by beauty and elevated or inspired intelligence imagines the beautiful object.

When we set out to create an object, first we must imagine what we wish to create. In our experience, the next step is taking action to make the object we desire. This is the way it works in this world of limitation. In the world of spirit, a new object is created instantly through the imaginative power of pure intelligence. For that vision to become a material reality, actions need to take place, fueled by desire. As the object to be created is the outer skin, so to speak, of the Creator's spirit, it is guided by an internal vision toward expressing its wholeness. Materialization of an idea does not proceed step-by-step as an engineer would carry it out. Rather, the object-to-be feels its way, responding to whatever influences it encounters while intuitively seeking its goal.

In the creative process, both accidental and intentional change can happen. Do the gene mutations of neo-Darwinian theory play the role of accident and the drive evident in the emerging of the embryo represent the intentional action of desire?

According to the view of mystics, the great drama of evolution revealed by the fossil record can be seen as the progressive development of instruments increasingly capable of supporting and expressing the nature of spirit. Intelligence and consciousness have always been present, seeking more capacity for expression, understanding, and appreciation by condensing into evermore complex and capable material forms. The modern belief is that humans belong to a tree of life from which we can trace our ancestry, at least schematically, back through primates, further to early mammals, and ultimately, to a common ancestor of all animals. However, the mystic sees it differently. It is the instrument we occupy that has evolved over eons to the human form. Our true nature is the living spirit that animates the instrument:

> Now when we come to the evolution of the world according to the point of view of the mystic, we shall see that it is not the human being who has come from the plant and animal and rock, but the human has taken

the body, the physical instrument from the rock, from the animal, from the plant. But we ourselves have come direct from the spirit and we are directly joined to the spirit. We are, will be, and always are above this instrument which we have borrowed from the earth. In other words, plainly speaking, the human being is not the product of the earth, but is the inhabitant of heavens. It is the body which we have borrowed from the earth. Because we have forgotten our origin, the origin of our soul, we have taken the origin of the earth which is only of our body and not of our soul.[6]

Pure intelligence is one and the same as spirit, the condition of unity underlying our experience of reality. Pure intelligence, as the observing Self, projects itself as rays into every object through the process of condensation, the materialization of spirit. In the mystic's view, the essential nature of a human is a ray of the original cosmic Self, the ray being the soul. The ray, no different from its source, but rather the source extending itself, adopts the instrument that evolution has prepared for it. However, the instrument is also spirit condensed into tangible form. The essential nature of the soul and the instrument are the same. One might say they are different phases of spirit, as steam, liquid water, and ice are different phases of one substance.

Through the sensorium of the instrument, the soul has a limited consciousness. However, the nature of the soul in every object from an electron to a crystal, to an amoeba, to a human is the same pure intelligence. The soul appears to be separate for each individual. The mystic perceives such separateness of an individual's soul to be an illusion.

The creation and the Creator are not two separate things. One is the outer life and the other the inner life of one real-

6. Hazrat Inayat Khan, *Complete Works, Original Texts: Lectures on Sufism*, 1926 II (New Lebanon, NY: Omega Publications, 2011), 294.

ity. In response to the idea that there is no God or Creator, existentialists bravely accept that the universe came about through random material causes, admittedly under the influence of elegant and orderly forces that have given rise to seemingly intelligently designed complex creatures. Further, they believe that any creative or purposeful actions are wholly the responsibility of humans. A mystic would say that the observed elegant order of the universe and the seemingly intelligent design of organisms are signs of an inherent intelligence that both underlies and is expressed through nature. Creative and purposeful actions undertaken by humans are not only individual acts but are expressions of a universal desire acting through all aspects of the universe. The Creator is an impulse of love seeking beauty and the universe is an outcome of that impulse.

6

Why Is There Evil in the World?

In 1755 a massive earthquake with an estimated magnitude of 8.5 to 9.0 struck several hundred miles off the coast of Portugal. The quake damage drove the crowds in Lisbon that were celebrating the Feast of All Saints down to the docks, but shortly afterward they were engulfed in a giant tsunami. Some 30,000 people lost their lives. This event shook the faith of believers in Europe. Among them was Voltaire, who expressed his doubts about the goodness of God in his *Poem on the Lisbon Disaster, or an Examination of the Axiom, "All is Well."*

> But how conceive a God supremely good,
> Who heaps his favors on the sons he loves,
> Yet scatters evil with as large a hand?
> What eye can pierce the depth of his designs?
> From that all-perfect Being came not ill:
> And came it from no other, for he's lord:
> Yet it exists. O stern and numbing truth![1]

An even more destructive tsunami off the coast of Indonesia in 2004 killed roughly 228,000 people along the coasts of Southeast Asia. Yet in modern times, though this tragedy was

---

1. Voltaire, "Poem on the Lisbon Disaster," trans. Joseph McCabe, https://en.wiki source.org/wiki/Toleration_and_other_essays/Poem_on_the_Lisbon_Disaster.

no less traumatic, it did not cause as great a stir in Western feelings about the goodness of God as the Lisbon disaster did.

In our time the question of theodicy, or how to explain evil if God exists, immediately brings up the Holocaust and a series of other contemporary genocides. Six million Jews died from 1941 to 1945, one and three quarters million Cambodians died under the Pol Pot regime from 1975 to 1979, and three quarters of a million or 70 percent of the Tutsi population of Rwanda died in 1994. If God exists and is omnipotent and all good, how could God let such tragedies befall so many innocent victims? Either God is not omnipotent and there is an evil force that competes with God, or God is not all good and is responsible for evil as well as good. Or, God is indifferent to human suffering. An atheist would say the answer is that God does not exist, so there is no need for an explanation. For an existentialist, the responsibility for good rests squarely on human shoulders.

The Story of Job

Job in the biblical story is an upright man, prosperous and well respected, with a happy family. God is fond of Job and points out his faithfulness to Satan who in this story seems to be a familiar companion of God. In his sly way, Satan questions whether Job would be so faithful if he didn't enjoy his privileged life. God, believing in Job's steadfastness and innocence, gives Satan permission to take away all of Job's comforts and expose him to suffering as a test to prove his unwavering faith. Not only does Job lose his wealth and family, but his health also deteriorates. He is subjected to continual anxiety, pain, and restless sleep. He curses the day he was born but doesn't curse God. His friends seek to console him but they assume God is benevolent, and therefore, Job must have done something to deserve his misery. Job insists that he is innocent and cries out to God for some explanation, for some greater understanding. He reproaches his friends, saying that instead of finding fault with him, they could have prayed for and supported him in seeking to understand.

Finally, God appears to Job. Instead of responding to Job's questions, God puts Job in his place by barraging him with overwhelming and intimidating questions such as, "Where were you when I laid the foundations of the earth?" Job acknowledges the power and sovereignty of God, responding, "I have heard of Thee by the hearing of the ear, but now my eye sees Thee. Therefore, I will keep silent, and repent in dust and ashes." God is impressed with Job's sincerity and loyalty. He heals Job's body, restores all he had lost, and gives him twice as much as he had before.

What does this story say about evil in the world? The simplest conclusion is that when evil happens to good people, it is a test of their faith. Can they be good when circumstances are horrendous? If it were only a test for proving how good they are, it would seem cruel and arbitrary. If the test were meant to bring out their best qualities, that would have greater meaning. But if they die as a result, or suffer lifelong grief or pain, what has been accomplished?

When things go wrong, the feeling often arises, "I must have done something to bring this about. There must be something wrong with me." This is the assumption Job's friends make about him. If one upholds one's self-respect, if one believes in one's innocence when one is innocent, does one draw to oneself the strength and magnetism that Job experienced in his audience with God?

If we assume that God is separate from ourself, we might see God in this story as a bully, intimidating Job when it was God who was responsible for the suffering Job justifiably questions. Carl Jung in *Answer to Job* views concepts of God as evolving through the influence of inherent archetypes on the human imagination. He concludes from the story of Job that a concept of God is evolving. God is in the wrong, and is learning something about Himself through his admiration for Job's moral rectitude.

What if we consider God as the ground of Being, that is, if we assume there is no separation between God and Job. Then, God is testing Himself and God is also Satan the tempter. Jung intuited that the tension in the story of Job is related to the tension in our psyche between what he called the shadow and the conscious self. We avoid what is in the shadow by pushing it into the unconscious because we are uneasy about it. Is the shadow evil? In the story of Job, Satan is the shadow of God. God has two sides. This shadow nature of God can be traced back to the origin of Self when pure intelligence drew itself into a center.

The primal Self contains the seed of the *nafs*, the little self or ego of the individual. As long as the primal Self is only aware of its subject, the seeds of the *nafs* are dormant. In its desire to know itself, the Self must project itself onto objects, thus setting up a primary three-part form of relationship: the knower, the knowing, and the known. Inherent in this triple nature of experience is duality, namely between the self and the other. The negative aspects of self or ego—jealousy, resentment, hatred, grudge-holding, violent urges, lust, greediness—arise from the reaction the self has to the existence of another self.

When evil manifests in human nature or human events, as also noted in relation to the shadow nature of God, the shadow nature of the ego can be traced back to Self, the source of self. In other words, God is responsible. By the same token, all the heroic, noble, and chivalrous aspects of the self are also present in the nafs or seed of ego. These play out in altruistic responses to evil in human affairs. God is not absent when these things happen. God is present on both sides. God is oppressor and liberator, witness, forgiver, and revenge taker. God cannot be only good and whole. God has a unitary nature, a dualistic nature, and a triune nature.

Krishna's Advice to Arjuna in the Bhagavad Gita

Arjuna, the son of Indra, was the great warrior among the Pandava brothers. The eldest brother, Yudishthira, was in line to succeed the king of their homeland. The cousins of the Pandavas, the Kauravas, headed by Duryodhana, harbored feelings of jealousy and rivalry toward the Pandavas. By magic and trickery, Duryodhana caused the Pandavas to go into exile for twelve years in the forests. The years of tension and antagonism that preceded the exile prepared the way for an inevitable war between the families when the Pandavas returned. Now the battle is about to be joined. Two armies face each other. Arjuna surveys the scene and feels cast down and defeated. In the ranks of the enemy, he sees his mentors, great warriors he not only respects but reveres. In the prospect of victory, he sees great loss. He cries out to his charioteer who happens to be Krishna, an avatar of Vishnu.

Krishna gives Arjuna this advice:

Thy tears are for those beyond tears; and are thy words words of wisdom? The wise grieve not for those who live; and they grieve not for those who die—for life and death shall pass away.

Because we all have been for all time: I, and thou, and those kings of men. And we all shall be for all time, we all for ever and ever.

As the Spirit of our mortal body wanders on in childhood, and youth and old age, the Spirt wanders on to a new body: of this the sage has no doubts. . . .

The unreal never is: the Real never is not. This truth indeed had been seen by those who can see the true.[2]

2. *The Bhagavad Gita*, 2:11–13, 16, trans. Juan Mascaro (Middlesex, UK: Penguin Books, 1962).

Arjuna takes courage from these words, and the battle results in a victory for the Pandavas.

If we take these words of Krishna as the wisdom of mystical insight, what implications do they have for our relationship with evil in the world? What does it mean to apply these ideas to the genocides of the Holocaust and in Cambodia, Rwanda, and other lands? If we had Krishna's insight, would we take the loss of so many innocent lives as an illusion? Would we be able to say that life lives, and it is death that dies, that those who have died go on living in another realm? Krishna is saying spirit never dies. He is appealing to Arjuna to follow his dharma or destiny despite the grief and loss that will ensue. Were the terrible tragedies of the twentieth century destined to happen? In our grief for innocent lives lost and grotesque injustice, are we missing the destiny of souls that will go on beyond this life, continuing from where they left off, presumably in a better place? For those mystics who have achieved a high degree of indifference and therefore freedom from the suffering inherent in life in this world, these words signify deep faith in the rightness of all that happens. It is a surrender and acceptance that is not a resignation, not a great sigh, of "Oh well." Rather, it is an unshakable belief that everything happens for a reason and the glaring injustices of this life are resolved when all the causes and implications can be grasped in a much larger perspective.

Still, for most of us, any words or ideas that attempt to explain away the horrors of genocide, outbreaks of senseless violence, the oppression of minorities, or the brutality of tyrants, seem like a heartless and insensitive travesty. Evil has not only inflicted cruel suffering on its victims but has left in its wake the broken hearts of those who have survived it.

The Trial of God

Theodicy challenges one's belief in God. For those who have been imbued by a religious tradition with a belief in God, the question, "Why does God not intervene when evil arises?" can bring about feelings of despair. Elie Wiesel, as a Jewish youth caught in the nightmare of the Holocaust, witnessed a small group of rabbis in a concentration camp meeting to put God on trial. After solemn consideration, they found God guilty, then adjourned to say the evening prayers.

Wanting to examine his own feelings about putting God on trial, Wiesel wrote the play *The Trial of God* which takes place in the eighteenth century in a tiny Jewish settlement in Russia. The play's characters are celebrating Purim, a remembrance of the miraculous rescue of the Jews by Queen Esther when Haman—the evil advisor to the emperor—plotted to kill all Jews in the Persian Empire. Purim is sometimes celebrated by putting on a spiel or play, often of a comic or satiric nature. In Wiesel's play, the Jews celebrating Purim are survivors of a recent pogrom that slaughtered many in their village. A warning of an imminent second pogrom hangs over the proceedings. They choose to enact a trial of God as their Purim play. A mysterious stranger calling himself Sam shows up to play the part of the defense attorney. The prosecutor, the innkeeper Berish, is embittered by the last pogrom and passionately presents it as evidence against God. Berish begins his indictment:

> I accuse Him of hostility, cruelty and indifference. Either He dislikes His chosen people or He doesn't care about them—period! But then, why has He chosen us—why not someone else, for a change? Either He knows what's happening to us, or He doesn't wish to

know! In both cases He is . . . He is . . . guilty! (*Pause.
Loud and clear*) Yes, guilty![3]

Sam makes the traditional arguments in defense of God.
It was human evil that was responsible for the pogrom, not
God. Berish counters by asking: if God is a neutral bystander, does he not care about what is happening? Sam replies
that God is suffering along with the victims. Berish asks if
this means God is powerless. Berish says he speaks for the
victims. Sam says Berish can't know what the victims have
experienced. What if they were happy to leave this life behind for something better? What if by dying they became
closer to God? Besides, God's ways are beyond our understanding. God has a reason for evil that we can't comprehend. Sam claims that the dead have seen God's grace and
they are at peace. Sam says that those who were spared have
something to be thankful for. Berish is appalled. He is left
with bitterness. Sam says that Berish hurts God by his un-
gratefulness. Sam appeals to tradition. What of those Jews
who suffered the persecutions of the past and remained
faithful nevertheless to God? Why is it different now? Who
are you, Berish, to speak against God? Berish responds in
the spirit of existentialism. He will speak for those in the past
who kept quiet. He takes responsibility as a human agent.
He will speak the truth to authority and not be intimidated.
Humans cannot look to God for justice. They have to take
responsibility for it themselves. Sam responds with the words
of faith—God created him to serve God and to glorify God.
God can do whatever he pleases with those he has created.
Sam sums up his arguments:

---

3. Elie Wiesel, *The Trial of God* (New York: Schocken Books, 1979), 125.

It's simple. Faith in God must be as boundless as God Himself. If it exists at the expense of man, too bad. God is eternal, man is not.[4]

In the trial, the judge is played by Mendel. He is so impressed by Sam's statements and his solid faith that he takes him to be a holy man, a tzaddik. Berish is repulsed by Sam's arguments. Before a judgment can be made, sounds of the impending anticipated pogrom are heard. At the end of the play, Sam reveals his true identity as Satan, laughing as the roars of the soldiers grow louder.

Sam's traditional arguments mirror the sentiments of Job's friends. They ignore the enormity of injustice in the persecution of the innocent. Instead, they appeal to God's greatness, acknowledge human smallness, and call for submission. They seem to affirm the medieval feudal attitude of fealty. However, the protection that is expected from the lord in the feudal relationship is postponed to a future condition in an afterlife. We are supposed to take, on faith, that there is a greater meaning behind events than we can understand. This is cold comfort to those who have suffered great loss or who see values and principles trampled upon, seemingly with impunity. Though the wisdom spoken by Krishna may be true, it is no more than empty words to those who have been burned by cruelty and horror. For mystical insights to be meaningful and consoling, one has to experience them firsthand, as one often also hears in NDE testimonials, after which one no longer fears death.

4. Ibid., 157.

Reb Zalman Confronts the Holocaust

Theodicy's glaring example of the Holocaust has undermined the belief in God of many Jews. Reb Zalman
Schachter, a well-known founder of the Jewish Renewal
movement, traces this disaffection to a deep psychological
issue: we are angry that God did not ask us if we wanted to
be created. We had no choice about being alive and exposed
to the risk of traumatic experiences. This seems unfair. To
deal with this angry feeling, he suggests a confrontation with
the Creator.

> I have found that the only thing that helps is to take the
> time to tell the Master of the Universe that our greatest
> anger is in that He made us without our consent. After
> all, we didn't make ourselves. I can't express genuine
> love to God or fellow beings if there is always a lid on
> my anger. I can say to God, "You're beautiful, You're
> marvelous, and I love You, and I'm glad I live in Your
> world," only after I have had a chance to tell Him of
> my rage. No one who hasn't taken a vigil for a night
> and had it out with ribbono shel olam, can get to a
> place where faith becomes real.[5]

Reb Zalman suggests three ways we can relate to God: as
It, as He/She, or as Thou. As It, God is infinite and inscru-
table. As an individual self, one can't have any relationship
with God as It. Zalman's He/She God is distant and mor-
ally neutral toward human concerns. This is also Spinoza's
God whose greatness is perceived in the laws of nature. One
would be self-centered and parochial to think this God cares
about human welfare. God as Thou allows an intimate rela-

5. Rabbi Zalman Schachter, *The Spirituality of the Future*, The Shalom Center,
2008, https://theshalomcenter.org/node/1395.

tionship with God. To have a relationship, God has to accept a limitation or restraint to give us space for free will.

> That God can be Thou means that God must be infinity-minus something. The problems as well as the possibilities of the world lie in the reality that there should be a minus one, that God contracts Her/Himself so that others can exist for whom God is Thou. But, out of that fantastic self-limitation of the infinite God comes the possibility of evil, the randomness, the chaotic element in our experience.[6]

This is where evil arises. It comes from the possibility of our free will. If God were to interfere whenever free will causes hurt or harm, we wouldn't really have free will. To have free will means there is the possibility of making mistakes, little ones and very big ones. The consequences may be horrific, but that is the price we have to pay for having the capacity to choose.

There is a greater meaning to suffering. How do we learn and grow in our lives? It is not so much through happy experiences. They reinforce the status quo. It is through pain and trouble that we become wiser. We learn empathy for the pain of others. We learn to care about others and not just our own welfare. We learn to expand and open our hearts and forgive.

> Sometimes suffering exists in order to bring us to our senses. Sometimes suffering exists in order to show us that there are tragedies we can't overcome with our childish omnipotence in the world. We begin to see that every choice we make has its consequences. Suffering is the way in which we learn, after the fact, the consequences of our moves.[7]

6. Ibid.
7. Ibid.

A Mystical View of Theodicy

A mystic seeks to understand life and reality by discovering the unity that underlies pairs of opposites. When it comes to good and evil, the mystical point of view is that evil is the shadow of good. As shadow is an effect, not a reality, evil does not exist for the mystic. How can one see the unity underlying the duality of good and evil? We readily recognize actions that are good and beneficial. We can also think of actions that are less good but which we still consider good. We can continue down the scale to actions that are good but have some bad consequences. Then, as we proceed, we find actions that are increasingly bad. Compared to a very bad action, a mildly bad action might be considered relatively good. For any action we consider to be bad, we can always find a worse action in comparison to which the first action is better. Rather than dividing our evaluation of actions between good and bad, we could place all actions on a continuous scale from very much good to very little good. Evil, then, is a shadow whose darkness is a measure on a scale of good.

The mystic sees the bad in the good and the good in the bad. Situations are always complex. They are never all good or all bad. Sometimes a good situation has unforeseen consequences that are bad and vice versa. Judging whether a situation is good or bad depends on how it is viewed. From one angle a situation may look promising, while from another angle one may see flaws and dangers. One's perspective on a situation depends on one's knowledge of the circumstances. There may be many layers of unresolved historical and cultural nerve filaments threading through a situation that many would miss. Recognizing that in our ordinary experience we learn to judge things by how they affect us, the mystic does not allow a self-interested perspective to take God to task. A mystic tries to remain open to the possibility that there is a much larger point of view informed by eons of experience that accounts for how things unfold, even if events seem to our narrow horizon harsh and unjust.

To a mystic, the apparent injustice in the behaviors of those who seek to take advantage or misuse others is contradicted by the action of conscience. It has been said that every day is Judgment Day. Those who think they can get away with spurning the moral code must live with a conscience that judges and punishes them. Is there a universal moral code? For a mystic, whatever gives peace is good and whatever disturbs peace is wrong. Those who disturb the peace of others or of nature have to live with the consequences of their actions. They will not be able to find peace in themselves. Those who bring about peace for others or harmony in nature immediately feel the reward within. This justice is continually meted out not by an external judge who rewards or punishes but by the inner nature of every actor on the stage of life. The cynic may feel that life is basically unfair, while the mystic sees justice fulfilled in every direction.

How do we know what is right or wrong? If there were no shadow of evil, how would we know what good is?

> The miseries and wickedness of humanity do not come from good, but good comes out of wickedness and miseries. If it were not for wickedness and miseries and wrong we would never have appreciated what good and right mean. It is the idea of these two opposite poles which makes us able to distinguish between the two qualities.[8]

How does wickedness come about? Jung pointed out the existence of the shadow in our psyche, the suppressed impulses of unrestrained self-interest. Those impulses might

8. Hazrat Inayat Khan, "Pairs of Opposites," in *Sufi Teachings*, vol. VIII, *The Sufi Message of Hazrat Inayat Khan* (Katwijk: Servire, 1963), 101.

arise from appetites such as sexual lust or lust for power, or they might arise from fears and insecurities such as jealousy or resentment. According to the mystic, our essence or soul comes straight from a state of perfection, while the instrument of the body, mind, and heart is by nature limited. Our conditioned self, the personality in which we function, is limited and fears death. Self-preservation is our priority, not only to survive physically but also to feel secure and self-confident. Evil arises when selfish impulses reign free or when fears and insecurities dominate behavior. When one begins to realize the conditioned self that wants everything for itself is only a construct held in the mind and there is a real self inside the conditioned self that gets satisfaction from serving others, one finds in one's true nature an innate goodness. The mystic believes that the nature of perfection is good and right, while wrong comes about through limitation. Is God then all good? Yes, in its perfect form. However, God is also the motive force in the world of limitation. In that sense, God includes right and wrong, good and evil.

Why must we endure suffering and go through the struggles of life? When we go to a play, we are entertained by the tensions, conflicts, and denouement at the end. Something has been gained by going through the turmoil of the drama. Someone has to play the victim and someone the villain, someone plays the hero or heroine, and someone plays the sidekick or bystander.

It is the same with God and the Creation. The whole of manifestation is arranged, with all its desirable and undesirable aspects, with its right and wrong, and with all the kindness and cruelty that we see on the surface of this earth; all this produces in the end one single effect for which the whole play was made. One might say that if this is only a play then it is nothing, but if this is nothing, then there is nothing else that we can call anything. If anything exists at all, it is this manifestation; one may call it everything or nothing, as one wishes.[9]

In the mystical perspective, God and humans are not separate. Whatever we go through in life, God also goes through the same. If God intervenes, it is through the presence of God in manifestation. God may be in the charismatic person who turns the tide or in the change of heart in the general who withdraws his troops. God might be in the faithful dog who chases off predators while a key person lies helpless on the ground. On the other side of the coin, God may be the passion in the tyrant who oppresses his subjects or the rage in the killer driven by raw emotional wounds. The outflowing of love is pouring through channels of all sizes, under great tension through constricted ditches, overflowing banks where capacity is limited, or nurturing meadows that soak up its bounty. Disaster and catastrophe tear down the ego's resistance leaving in its wake grief and bitterness or freedom and wisdom. For the mystic, the drama is accomplishing a goal. It is teleological, goal oriented. Chaos moves toward order, love moves toward beauty. Chaos and ugliness have their roles to play and their players. What is accomplished by the play is not readily seen. Amid the drama, we are dismayed or despairing or bewildered. In the end, it is the soul, our unlimited essence, that will be satisfied. If our soul is not awake, we can't reach that satisfaction, and must abide with whatever we feel, and hope that one day we will understand.

---

9. Hazrat Inayat Khan, "Art, Yesterday, Today, and Tomorrow," in *The Path of Initiation*, vol. X, *The Sufi Message of Hazrat Inayat Khan* (London: Barrie and Rockliff, 1964), 232.

Pause for Reflection

We have examined three important issues that arise in the mind of a skeptical person impressed with scientific materialism and questioning traditional teachings of religion. Science and philosophy have attempted to grapple with these issues. We have also considered another point of view, namely, what those who have explored the inner life, the mystics, have to say. In doing so, we have encountered a way of understanding reality that is quite different from our usual perspective.

The idea of pure intelligence as a form of intelligence that is absolute rather than relative, that is the essence of oneself and every person, that can't be compared between people is distinct from our usual notion of intelligence. It is based on the idea that there is such a thing as perfection. In traditional Western religion, perfection is a quality of God. Perfection doesn't fit into our ordinary notion of reality, in which everything is limited or imperfect. Intellectually, perfection can be understood as a limiting case. We can imagine an object, for example, a rose, that is increasingly perfect with time. As close as it comes to being perfect, it is still limited. There is always something we can find in it that is imperfect.

Cosmic idealism is another example that departs from usual notions of reality. It says that reality is based in the mind of the universe or God. An existentialist would say that everything is given, there is no rhyme or reason for the way things are. Life just is the way it is, as objective empiricism shows it to be. There are mechanical reasons for how everything has come about. Cosmic idealism, however, says that outer reality is a projection of inner reality, of the thoughts and feelings of a cosmic entity. It is the mind of one entity that creatively imagines all we observe in nature and all we discover internally.

When we explored the questions of how this universe came about and was there a Creator, we considered the mystical point of view called nondual reality. The Creator creates from its own Self. The creation is not separate from the Creator. This view differs from our everyday way of looking at the world called dualism.

The unitary point of view also came up in the examination of theodicy. If reality is unified, then all opposites are an illusion. Goodness and evil do not imply two opposed beings, God and Satan. If God exists, then God must encompass both good and evil. God cannot be complete and whole and all good. All experience must in some way originate from one source.

All these examples refer back to a nondual understanding of reality, whereas our ordinary experience demonstrates to us a dualistic reality. To go beyond the dualism of our everyday experience requires great discipline, training, and experience in quiet listening or meditation. Those who have devoted their lives to inner exploration have reported that a convincing experience of unity comes about with sufficient attention to the inner life.

Part 3 is an examination of the implications of the nondual perspective on the meaning of the word "God."

Part 3

The One

7

The Nondual Perspective

There is One Individual hidden behind many individuals; there is One Person shining through all personalities.

—Hazrat Inayat Khan, "Talas," in *Vadan*

IT SEEMS OBVIOUS that each of us is an isolated individual surrounded by innumerable objects. When we are alienated, other people can seem like objects. Yet, we can be close to others we care for. When our heart is open to another, we recognize that seeing the other as an object is a superficial view. If our feeling of isolation, of separation from others, is the surface of our perspective, what would a deeper perspective be? As we open our heart and allow feelings of warmth, of affection, of admiration, of love for another to arise, the feeling of separation is reduced. We recognize in another similar feelings to our own. We feel close to the one we love. We wish to be closer; we even wish to unite with the other. Experiencing love may also heighten feelings of loneliness and put us in touch with an underlying desire to be fully seen and loved.

As we have explored, we are accustomed to a way of seeing the world that is called dualism. It is the way our brain works. We experience ourselves as subject and everything else as object. When we have an intense connection with another, perhaps as a parent and child or a couple absorbed in love, there may be moments when we so deeply sympathize with the other that we get into their consciousness. We see through their eyes. In those moments, we see the one we love as subject rather than object. The barrier that seems to separate us, for that moment, goes away. For that moment, we are united with the other. Our dualistic way of seeing is temporarily replaced by merging into unity.

Another way to understand the difference between the surface and the depth of our perspective is to consider what we mean by essence. On the surface, we take for granted what our senses present to us. We objectify whatever is before us. We see what is before us with the eye of the intellect. If we go deeper, we begin to see what is before us with the eye of the heart. It is difficult to see the essence of what is before us.

Let's begin by asking ourselves, "What is the essence of my self?" Is that essence my body, mind, feelings, personality, consciousness? Essence is not changeable. My body, mind, feelings, and personality have all changed in my lifetime. They are continually changing. What about my consciousness? It, too, changes from sleeping to waking, from drowsy to alert, and between many states. If I strip away my identity with the body, mind, feelings, personality, and consciousness, what is left? There is a bare sense of "I" that remains that does not depend on any other form of identity. That bare sense of "I" is associated with an intuition of intelligence distinct from the personal intelligence we are accustomed to. It is simply a capacity to understand, not requiring any content.

If this is our experience of essence, is it not the same essence anyone would recognize in themselves? From this depth of perspective, the essence of every person appears to be the same. We are not in actuality separate beings but are linked by having the same essence. The mystic would go further, saying that the capacity of intelligence associated with our essential "I" is universal. In other words, the essence of everything is the same impersonal capacity for intelligence.

Contrasted with the dualism we experience on the surface, there is another way of understanding in the depths called the nondual perspective. In the essence of things, there is only subject, no object. And there is only one subject.

Implications of the Nondual Perspective

Our way of thinking and use of language are based on the way our dualistic brain works. We describe things by comparing them with something else. We can discriminate between things only when they are distinct. Dualistic thinking is based on contrast, such as, "This mountain is bigger than that hill." The nondual perspective says there is only one underlying essence that can't be compared with anything because it is unique. Being the essence of everything, there is nothing to compare it with. Those who have encountered a state of unity say it is indescribable.

In the dualistic perspective, we make comparisons. In mathematics, for any number there is always a larger number: that number plus one. From the dualistic viewpoint, for any object, person, or quality, one can always imagine a more perfect instance. For any person you think of who is kind, you can always imagine a kinder person. Limitation is the nature of the dualistic way of being. The essence, however, of any feature or quality is nondual. Being singular, it can't be compared with anything. Since it can't be improved upon, it is perfect as it is. In the nondual perspective, one finds the hidden perfection behind the appearance of limitation.

In the dualistic world, everything is continually changing. Nothing is spared. With living things, there is birth and the freshness of youth, the fullness of maturity, and the decline of aging, followed by death. Life proceeds in cycles as can be seen in the seasons or the transition from one generation to the next. Inorganic life abides by the law of entropy: the energy of any system degrades over time to its lowest possible state unless it is renewed by an outside source. On the other hand, the nature of essence is that it is unchanging. For a system that never changes, time—which can only be measured by change—has no meaning. Therefore, from the nondual perspective, essence is eternal. Eternal in this case does not mean stretching out in time forever. Time disappears. There is only the eternal now.

Our experience of separation and dualistic perspective of objects spread out over varying distances gives us an experience of space. Our sense of space depends on the ability to discriminate here from there. In the nondual perspective, there is no separation. As universal subject, I am here and there and everywhere. I discover my essence as a universal sense of "I" that could also be described as pure or perfect intelligence with no definite location in space. There is no place where it is not present. As there is no discrimination of place, space becomes meaningless in the nondual perspective. The universal "I" is all-pervading. Wherever you look, there it is.

Monotheism

Western religions are zealous in proclaiming there is one God. In part, this reflects the historical struggle against polytheism. In early societies, it was common practice to worship a variety of gods that were responsible for different aspects of life. These household gods were familiar and reassuring. They were present in the home in the form of idols and were believed to be watching over each family's everyday needs. The story of Abraham smashing the idols in his father's workshop and Muhammad breaking the idols stored at the Kaaba in Mecca illustrate the vehemence with which the Abrahamic religions affirm one God.

In Christianity, the affirmation of one God is captured in the Nicene Creed: "We believe in one God, the Father Almighty, Maker of heaven and earth, and of all things visible and invisible." In Judaism, this belief is expressed in the Shema: "Hear, O Israel: the Lord our God, the Lord is one" (Deuteronomy 6:4). And in Islam, the shahada also expresses this belief: "There is no god but God. Muhammad is the messenger of God."

These affirmations of monotheism declare that there is one God, not a variety of gods. There is also a deeper meaning in these declarations. The Shema, in Hebrew, is written: Sh'ma Yisrael Adonai Eloheinu, Adonai Ehad. Here, the word *ehad* declares one God. The word *ehad* means not only numerically one, it also means oneness. God is oneness or unity. God is nondual. To describe God, the Qur'an uses the Arabic word *ahad* corresponding to the Hebrew word *ehad*. There is a story that in the early days of Islam, some rabbis heard about a new religion and asked the Prophet about the meaning of God in Islam. Muhammad told them he would give them an answer after some reflection. Then, he received the revelation called Sura Ikhlas, sincerity or purity (sura 112). The Arabic version of this short sura is:

Qul hu Allah hu Ahad Allah hu Samad
Lam yalid wa lam yulad wa lam yakun
Lahu kufuwan Ahad
Say God is oneness, God is eternal
God is neither born nor does God give birth
And there is none like unto God.

This sura gives expression to what Muslims call *tawhid*, God's absolute oneness. God is not only absolute oneness (*ahad*) but also unchanging essence (*samad*). God has no origin. The creation that springs from God is never separate from the Creator. As God is unique, One Being, there is no way to describe God. Nothing can be compared to God, nothing is "like" God.

Chapter 8

Wahdat al Wujud

AMONG THE MYSTICS called Sufis there is a vision of reality called *wahdat al wujud*, the unity of existence. Though it didn't originate with him, Ibn 'Arabi, a great Sufi mystic of the thirteenth century, was most instrumental in elaborating this vision. The word *wujud* refers to the existence of all things. However, Ibn 'Arabi reserved *wujud* for the primary existence belonging solely to God. All the phenomena we observe in the world, the constitution and life of the universe, are borrowed from the *wujud* of the One. The *wujud* or existence in phenomena is God's disclosure, or God revealing itself.

The divine qualities (*sifat*) constitute the bridge that governs the relationship between God and the universe. In simpler terms, we could say that absolute oneness, the Only Being, is the essence of existence. By virtue of its eternal nature or permanence, oneness is the only true reality. However, reality as essence at the core of Being has a surface that is constantly in flux. The essence loans its existence to the surface and the surface serves as a medium for the creative expression of the core reality. The philosophy of *wahdat al wujud* has been criticized as a form of pantheism, a reduction of the unlimited nature of God to its presence underlying nature. Ibn 'Arabi's version clearly envisions God as unlimited and primary while nature or the universe is understood as a contingent phenomenon.

A concise explication of *wahdat al wujud* is found in the work, *Risale-t-ul-wujudiyyah*, also known as "*Whoso Knoweth Himself . . .*" or *Know Yourself.* The work is attributed to Ibn 'Arabi but may instead be authored by Awhad al-din Baly-ani. It is a discourse on a saying of the Prophet, "Whoso knoweth himself, knoweth his Lord." It begins by bringing out the paradox that appears when trying to express oneness in dualistic language:

> He is, and there is not with Him any before or after, above or below, closeness or distance, how or where or when, time or moment or duration, manifested exis-tence or place. And He is now as He has always been. He is the one without oneness and the single without singleness. He is not composed of name and named, for His name is Him and His named is Him and there is no name or named other than Him. He is the first without firstness and the last without lastness. He is the apparent without appearance and the hidden without hiddenness.[1]

The best way to refer to the One is through negatives: what it is not. So we begin with no before or after, no close-ness or distance, and so on. Any description of the One limits its uniqueness. Therefore, it can be one and single, while not being aptly portrayed by descriptive words like "oneness" or "singleness." Names are but covers over its reality. What is named is particular and not universal.

When the One is referred to as He or Him, the language sounds like the religious tradition of a personal God and may bring up associations with a vision of God as dominating,

---

1. *Know Yourself*, trans. Cecelia Twinch (Cheltenham, UK: Beshara Publications, 2011), 17.

demanding, and judging. In Arabic, the word "he" is rendered by "hu." "Hu" also has the sacred meaning of Presence. We are able to sense the presence of another without looking to see who is behind us. What if we imagined near to us the presence of our most prized ideal: kind, loving, generous, honest, and pure. Imagine the security and peace we would feel with that loving presence always nearby. That impression begins to give a sense of the meaning of Hu as Presence.

Those who are called spiritual seekers are motivated to find union with the One. They may use the practice of meditation, hoping to stop the restlessness of the mind. By achieving a degree of mental silence, they aspire to open themselves to a deeper experience, possibly expecting to encounter a blissful or ecstatic vision. As long as one imagines that one—as an individual—may find the One or God, one is missing a crucial element of surrender as described in the following passage:

> No one sees Him except Himself, no one reaches Him except Himself and no one knows Him except Himself. He knows Himself through Himself and He sees Himself by means of Himself. No one but He sees Him. His veil is His oneness since nothing veils Him other than Him. His own being veils Him. His being is concealed by His oneness without any condition.[2]

Our longing to go beyond ourself stands in the way of the desire that underlies our desire. Our longing is motivated by the longing of Presence to know itself. When we meditate, we can never reach our goal if we imagine that we as an individual can attain knowledge of the One. It is only the One who can find the way to an experience of Presence by means of our meditation. It is the Presence that discovers

2. Ibid., 19.

itself through one's meditation. The One is the only reality. Therefore, only the One can see itself.

Why does the One veil itself in these ways? Our dualistic minds are incapable of perceiving the One. The oneness of Hu hides it from our sight. We understand things only by their condition. Since there is no way to gain a purchase on oneness by gripping on to a condition, it slips out of our grasp.

By the way, notice the paradox in the statement, "His veil is His oneness," when previously it was said, "He is the one without oneness." This is a trick of dualistic thinking. We can't talk about the One without using dualistic knowledge, even though we have already denied that it applies.

The title of the work cites a saying of Prophet Muhammad. Here is how the author explains the meaning of the Prophet's statement:

> the Prophet, God bless him and give him peace, said, "Whoever knows their self, knows their Lord." He also said, "I knew my Lord through my Lord." What the Prophet pointed out by that, is that you are not you but you are Him and there is no you. It is not that He enters into you or that you enter into Him, or that He comes out of you or that you come out of Him. That does not mean that you have being and you are qualified by this or that attribute. What is meant is that you never were and never will be, whether through yourself or through Him or in Him or with Him. You have neither ceased to be nor are you existent. You are Him and He is you, without any of these imperfections. If you know your existence in this way, then you know God, and if not, then not.[3]

This is a radical statement said in the plainest and most direct terms. It goes against what seems most evident to us.

3. Ibid., 20.

Isn't it obvious that each of us exists as a unique individual? If we have never existed and will never be, what is this life about, and for whom is this mystical treatise written? When the author says, "you never were and never will be," he is referring to our conditioned self, the self-image we have adopted that has been shaped by years of impressions we have gathered. We see our self in a certain way, and we think we know another person who is close to us. Our knowledge of our self and of another consists of concepts. We may discover tomorrow new and unexpected things about our self or the other person. Every person is a world and a mystery. Our self-concept and our concept of another is inadequate. In that sense, it is not real. We can know the surface, but we can't know the essence. The essence is real; it truly exists. The surface concept is a representation. It exists in our mind but has no independent or objective existence. My self-concept exists only in my mind. My self, as experienced by another, exists only in the other's mind and is not the same as my self-concept. However, the essence of me does exist and when I come to know that essence, I will know my Lord because my Lord is the Only Being existing as the essence of every person.

Poetically, the author refers to the essence of the One as "His face." We see by looking into a face the soul of a person. If we see a person from behind, it is difficult to identify the person. If we see their face, we recognize the person's uniqueness.

> Everything passes away except His face, both outwardly and inwardly. This means that there is no existent but Him. Nothing other than Him has being and therefore has to pass away so that His face remains. There is nothing except His face.

It is as if a person who does not know something, then comes to know it. Their existence does not disappear, but their ignorance disappears. Their existence remains as it was, without being exchanged for another, and without the existence of the ignorant person being added to, or mixed with, the knowing person: ignorance simply disappears.[4]

Our search to gain deeper knowledge means letting go of the ignorance of thinking that our self-concept is something real. We don't have to get rid of what we think is our self, because it has never existed. We don't invite in a divine Self to take the place of the small self. Rather, we stay as we have been all along. Our mistake is revealed to us, a case of mistaken identity. Then, we realize that we are His face, the most perfect expression of the Self, marveling at its existence and its nature.

4. Ibid., 27.

9

Unity as Viewed by a Scientist

DAVID BOHM, A renowned physicist and major contributor to the fields of quantum mechanics and relativity theory, had wide-ranging interests. He felt that the root problem in social and world affairs is fragmentation, the way we identify ourselves that splits us off from others and from those close to us, and even perhaps from parts of ourselves. His book *Wholeness and the Implicate Order* examines this issue from many angles and advocates for a vision of wholeness as an alternative to fragmentation. Bohm believes that our health on all levels—personal, social, political, international, and environmental—depends on a shift in our world view.

> The notion that all these fragments are separately existent is evidently an illusion, and this illusion cannot do other than lead to endless conflict and confusion. Indeed, the attempt to live according to the notion that the fragments are really separate is, in essence, what has led to the growing series of extremely urgent crises that is confronting us today. . . . Individually there has developed a widespread feeling of helplessness and despair, in the face of what seems to be an overwhelming mass of disparate social forces, going beyond the control and

even the comprehension of the human beings who are caught up in it.[1]

From an early age, Bohm was fascinated with the experience of motion. As motion is continuous rather than a series of still frames, it presents a direct apprehension of a natural phenomenon that exhibits wholeness. As he analyzes our unsatisfactory habits of fragmentary thinking, the notion of flowing movement serves as a metaphor for how we could think or see the world differently.

Language

Bohm observes that the way we use language reinforces our perception of the world as fragmented. As an experiment, he considers a modified form of language—not intended to be practical—that implies a dynamic or flowing view of the world. His experimental language demonstrates how a different way of using words has a direct effect on how we think and perceive.

Typically, language is based on a subject-verb-object structure. Subject and object are perceived as separate and static entities. The dynamic or movement is carried by the verb. In Bohm's experiment, instead of saying, "a statement is relevant," for example, he invents a verb that carries the qualification in the object, namely, the relevance of the statement. Language thus reflects what happens in the mind.

The word "relevant" derives from a verb "to relevate," which has dropped out of common usage, whose meaning is "to lift" (as in "elevate"). In essence, "to relevate"

---

1. David Bohm, *Wholeness and the Implicate Order* (London and New York: Routledge Classics, 2005), 1–2.

means "to lift into attention," so that the content thus lifted stands out "in relief."[2]

To make apparent the activity of lifting something into attention, Bohm adds to the English language—in this case, reinstating an archaic word—a verb that emphasizes a sense of flow or motion, rather than appending a meaning to the object "statement."

> We then introduce the verb "to relevate." This means: "To lift a certain content into attention again, for a particular context, as indicated by thought and language."[3]

Now, instead of saying, "the statement is relevant," one can say, "I re-levate the statement."

Continuing, Bohm adds the verb "re-vidate" from the Latin verb for "to see," *videre*. Here, "to see" means not only to see an image but also to understand. From these two verbs, to "re-levate" and to "re-vidate," he creates the nouns "levation" and "vidation." Now, one can see how emphasis on the verb instead of the noun shifts one's attention from fragmentation (the relationship of objects) to wholeness (the flow of activity). The two verbs are not distinct but are interdependent.

> In an act of vidation, it is necessary to levate a content into attention, and in an act of levation, it is necessary to vidate this content. So the two movements of levation and vidation merge and interpenetrate.[4]

This kind of approach to language Bohm calls the *rheomode* because it emphasizes the continuity of flow (a rheostat

2. Ibid., 41–42.
3. Ibid., 44.
4. Ibid., 47.

allows a smooth continuous control over the flow of current.) When we say, "John looks at a river" our attention is drawn to John and river, and secondarily, we notice the activity of looking. In the rheomode, we might say, "Looking is going on in a continuous flow of events that include abstractions of the flow called John and river." Both John and the river are actually events in flux that we have abstracted into solidified objects. In relation to the river, from moment to moment, the water John sees is not the same. The river is an event in flux. It is constantly changing. John is also like a river, aging from one moment to the next. He is not the same John from moment to moment. We abstract from the actual flux by thinking of John as a fixed object.

Bohm's rheomode is an experiment in imagining a language that reinforces an impression of wholeness. It demonstrates how our typical use of language promotes a worldview of fragmentation.

Consciousness

Approaching the question of fragmentation versus wholeness from another angle, Bohm explores the relationship of physical reality to consciousness. He has already asserted that physical reality can be understood as a flux of becoming. Objects in this flux are viewed as dynamic abstractions like a vortex in a stream. Although the vortex has some persistence of its own, it is in actuality a formation in the stream's flow and not a fixed and separate object.

What about thought? Is thought a static object or is it a dynamic pattern in a flow of becoming? Thought depends on memory. If we want to think about something, we first gather from memory the elements we want to analyze. Bohm sees this as a mechanical process. Memories are static objects. However, thought can also include a creative process such as a sudden flash of insight. Something new is added to thought that is not mechanical. Intuition also adds something new to thought that is not available from memory. Bohm calls this process of novel thought intelligent perception. It doesn't come from memory. There is no conditioned source that can account for it. He concludes that it must come from the same flux of becoming that he believes accounts for physical reality.

> So, we see that the ground of intelligence must be in the undetermined and unknown flux, that is also the ground of all definable forms of matter. Intelligence is thus not deducible or explainable on the basis of any branch of knowledge (e.g., physics or biology). Its origin is deeper and more inward than any knowable order that could describe it.[5]

Going further, he examines the distinction between thought and the physical reality we perceive as independent of thought. We are not able to observe physical reality as directly independent of our thinking. What we perceive through our senses has to be processed through our thinking to make any sense. Our senses present to us a jumble of impressions—shapes, colors, sounds, smells, tastes—that have to be assembled into something that has meaning for us. As Kant pointed out, we can't perceive the thing-in-itself, independent of the processing of our sensations of it. We can't disentangle our thinking from our apprehension of reality. Any seemingly fixed and final explanation of reality is a projection of our thinking and therefore not final but provisional. Our thinking about reality is always limited.

Every scientific theory is understood as a model of reality, not to be confused with a definitive grasp of reality. As scientific study progresses, models are tested and improved or replaced. In Bohm's view, our understanding of the totality of

5. Ibid., 67.

reality, consciousness, and what appears to be independent of consciousness unfolds to us in a continual flow of becoming. It will never reach a final form. Our grasp of reality will always be fringed with mystery.

Implicate and Explicate States

Viewing the issue of wholeness versus fragmentation from another angle, Bohm speculates that the scientific fields of relativity and quantum mechanics that have challenged classical ideas of physics require a dramatic shift in perspective. He points out that the original scientific revolution challenged the perspective that the earth is at the center of the universe and the motions of the planets could be described as epicycles. Until the time of Copernicus, increasingly precise observations of the motions of planets required progressively complex adjustments to the existing model of rotating crystalline spheres and spheres attached to spheres. This model of epicycles could still account for the observations but only by stretching it to match new data. The idea that the earth moved around the sun with the planets, comets, and asteroids offered a much simpler model. Bohm wonders if, instead of trying to make the peculiarities of relativity theory and quantum mechanics fit our current perspective, there might be another way of seeing reality that would prove to be a simpler model.

Newton's demonstration that the orbit of the moon could be explained by the same law of gravitation that describes an apple falling from a tree showed that physical laws established on earth are universal. To visualize the working of those laws, Descartes introduced the familiar Cartesian coordinate system with its x, y, and z axes. This way of viewing reality emphasized the separation of objects and their relationships. The way a lens works illustrates this mode of perception. The lens maps a physical object onto an image. Every point on the image corresponds to a point on the object. Our everyday experiences often align with this way of perceiving.

Bohm points out two realms in contemporary physics where its view of reality breaks down. In the realm of velocities approaching the speed of light, Einstein showed that objects are not as they appear, the notion of a rigid object falls apart. The apparent size and shape of an object depends on the speed of the observer relative to the object. An object will be seen differently by two observers moving at different speeds. Although this effect is not noticeable at ordinary speeds, it is still present at a tiny scale. Thus, objects must be regarded as patterns of movement rather than as rigid and solid. Einstein recognized this problem and tried to replace the idea of solid objects with a unified field, in which objects are localized enhancements of the field and merge with the other objects at their peripheries. He envisioned objects as having no definite boundaries. Although Einstein was not able to construct a final version of a unified field theory, his idea of the universe as an undivided whole—every part merging into every other part—remains an implication of relativity theory.

The second problematic realm for physics according to Bohm is the submicroscopic world of atoms and elementary particles. The famous Heisenberg uncertainty principle of quantum mechanics states that the accuracy of measuring certain pairs of quantities for a particle, such as position and velocity or time and energy, has a fundamental limit. If one quantity of the pair is known accurately, the accuracy of the other must be uncertain. A common interpretation of this principle attributes the uncertainty in the location or momentum of an observed particle to an unavoidable disturbance by the observation itself. The photon or electron used to probe the object changes its location or velocity in an unpredictable way causing an irreducible uncertainty. Bohm argues that the observed object and the observer must be considered as parts of a pattern of interaction rather than as mutually interacting objects. In other words, rather than viewing the observer or instrument and observed object as separate entities that interact, quantum mechanics requires that we take the situation as an undivided whole. Up to this point Bohm's representation of quantum mechanics is not controversial.

To accommodate this implication of wholeness, Bohm goes further and suggests a new metaphor in place of the way a lens maps an object to an image point-by-point. The new metaphor must illustrate a mapping of undivided wholeness. This effect is illustrated in a hologram. To produce a hologram, a laser beam is split. Half of the beam passes around an object and then interacts with the other half of the beam, producing an interference pattern that is captured on film as a hologram. When a laser beam is passed through the hologram, a three-dimensional image of the object is formed. If the laser beam is passed only through a corner of the hologram, the same image is displayed with less definition because an interference pattern maps phase information of the two beams at each point in space to the whole hologram. Therefore, every part of the hologram is capable of producing the whole image. Conversely, each point on the hologram is mapped to the whole object (see fig. 7).

Using another metaphor for mapping wholeness, Bohm examines what happens to an ink spot dropped into a viscous fluid. When the fluid is spun in a centrifuge, the ink spot is drawn out into tracks that eventually spread throughout the fluid and disappear. If the fluid is then spun in the reverse direction, the ink spot notably reappears. The ink spot is mapped to the whole fluid, and any spot in the fluid is mapped to the ink spot. If one instead places drops of ink successively across a rotating fluid, they sequentially disappear. If the drops are spaced close together, reversing the rotation of the fluid will produce what appears to be a single drop moving across the fluid. Further, if one could drop

a.

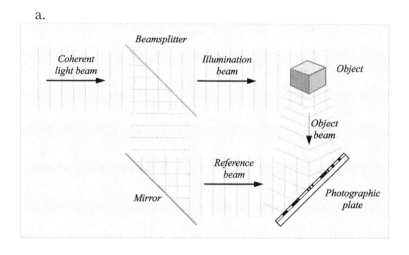

b.

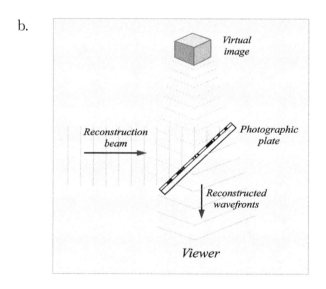

Figure 7. (*a*) Recording a hologram; (*b*) reconstructing a hologram. Image from DrBob at the English-language Wikipedia, https://en.wikipedia.org/wiki/Holography; licensed under the Creative Commons Attribution-Share Alike 3.0 Unported license.

a series of images successively on a rotating fluid and later reverse the rotation, one would view a moving picture, a simulation of a dynamic event.

Bohm calls the two modes of reality represented by the intact drop and the drop dispersed in the fluid explicate and implicate states. Turning the fluid one way implicates or interlaces the drop into the fluid, while turning the fluid the other way explicates or clarifies the fluid to reveal what has been hidden, returning it to the original form of a drop. He is suggesting a radically different view of reality. What we see and encounter in our experience is the explicate state of objects or entities, representing the familiar condition of separateness or fragmentation, comparable to the ink drop being distinctly visible on the fluid's surface. Bohm is suggesting that objects also exist in an implicate state in which they are "mapped" onto the "totality" or whole space. The implicate state is a hidden dimension of wholeness.

The image of a drop in a viscous fluid is a metaphor and not meant to be taken literally. Bohm is proposing that our ordinary experience of the world characterized by separateness or fragmentation is a surface or external aspect of the world. The world also has a deeper hidden aspect whose nature is undivided wholeness. He is proposing that there is a continual process of movement between these two states.

Bohm identifies flowing movement, also imagined as the unbroken state of becoming, as the essential nature of reality. This movement he calls the *holomovement*, the flowing movement of the totality. There is a continual flowing in the holomovement between the implicate state and the explicate state. As was true in the ink spot metaphor, what we witness may be the continual unfolding of a hidden reality rather than the persistence of an object. What appears to be a dynamic object may be a pattern of energy continually recreated by explication from an implicate state.

He believes that the laws of physics we can discern are valid for a particular realm. In another realm, there are other laws. Although all of the laws originate from the holomovement, we may never discover the underlying fundamental laws, rather, only how they express themselves in different realms.

To summarize, Bohm feels that the mysteries of relativity and quantum mechanics cannot be understood within the context of the current fragmented perspective of modern physics. Both theories imply an undivided wholeness that requires a radically different perspective. The mapping of the world of distinct and separate objects onto what he calls the totality is a radical attempt to conceptualize a relationship between our everyday dualistic way of understanding reality and the nondual reality of oneness. He is suggesting not only that physics can consider nondual wholeness as the essence of physical reality, but even that unresolved problems in modern physics require it.

Life and Consciousness

Bohm sees fragmentation in the ways we separate ourselves from others socially as well as in the way physicists divide the world into separate and independent parts such as atoms or elementary particles. He also sees fragmentation in the division we make between what is animate and inanimate and between matter and consciousness. He shows how the underlying unity of the holomovement in the implicate state can bind these dichotomies.

He has suggested that the fragmentation of matter is an abstraction of a more general state of holomovement. The primary state of matter is holographically distributed in the totality, referred to as the implicate state. In other words, the information of the whole universe is stored in every small region of space like a hologram, and the information for a particular object is spread throughout the universe. That information is enfolded or coded throughout space. When the information from a particular implicate state, such as the state of a particular ink drop, is unfolded, an object appears momentarily in the explicate state. The laws of its behavior in a particular realm, such as the macro realm of our daily experience or the micro realm of atoms, are approximations of more general universal laws that are relevant to the realm of observation.

Bohm notes that a plant grows from a seed based on the design information stored in its DNA. Guided by this information, the plant draws to itself the matter and energy it needs from its environment. How does life come into it? The scattered matter and energy that will constitute the plant is inanimate until it is assembled by the DNA of the plant. One could say that life is implicit in the ingredients of the plant and becomes explicit when it is incorporated into the plant. Drawing an analogy with the ink drop dispersed and then drawn back together, Bohm suggests that a plant draws its life from the totality. He infers that life is implicit in the holomovement. It is made explicit in a plant or other living organism and remains implicit in rocks and other inanimate objects. This idea removes the interpretation of fragmentation from the apparent split between animate and inanimate objects.

In relation to consciousness, Bohm considers what happens when we listen to music. We hear a succession of individual sounds that can be represented by notes on a page. In our experience of music, we are aware not only of sounds heard in the moment but also of their context of previous sounds held in memory. All sorts of associations may be aroused by the sounds, their sequence, and relationships. We respond to the sounds and associations with physical sensations and feelings. These responses combined constitute our experience of the music. This complex process passes through us as a continuous flow, mostly eluding our awareness. This example demonstrates what happens in our ordinary conscious experience. Bohm suggests that while listening to music, we have a direct experience of the implicate state or the holomovement. This type of description of subjective conscious experience seems included in what philosopher David Chalmers states is difficult for science to explain, the so-called hard problem of consciousness.

Bohm claims that matter and consciousness have a common core in the holomovement. Matter in the form of discrete objects and consciousness as the commonly experienced collection of thoughts and concepts are both explicated from the totality, a totality that is closely related to our subjective experience of consciousness.

A human being combines mind and matter, not as two separate systems, but as two interdependent and interacting projections from a common ground. A human being does not generally exist in isolation. The common ground that projects an individual also projects the multitude of individuals. One can picture a pond studded with many water-lily blossoms. If one dives beneath the surface, one sees many stems rising from a single plant.

> So it will be ultimately misleading and indeed wrong to suppose, for example, that each human being is an independent actuality who interacts with other human beings and with nature. Rather, all these are projections of a single totality. As a human being takes part in the process of this totality, he is fundamentally changed in the very activity in which his aim is to change that reality which is the content of his consciousness. To fail to take this into account must inevitably lead one to serious and sustained confusion in all that one does.[6]

6. Ibid., 266.

When Bohm says, "As a human being takes part in the process of this totality, he is fundamentally changed in the very activity in which his aim is to change that reality which is the content of his consciousness," I believe he is referring to the activity of thinking. One is trying to make progress with a thought, thinking through some content of the mind. The thinking process is not isolated to the circuits of the brain. It is influenced by sensations, feelings, memories, and influences of others. Bohm is suggesting that this complex process could be understood as the dynamic influence of the totality in its projection into the individual. In other words, thinking changes a person through a process that is visible in the explicate state and is hidden in the implicate state.

Bohm shows how to formulate an image of reality that is not fragmented but unified. The mysteries of modern physics seem to require a context of wholeness. The relationships between animate and inanimate matter and between matter and consciousness are two classic problems that benefit from similar treatment. Bohm intuits that continuous movement is more fundamental than the mechanistic interaction of independent objects. He identifies the flux of becoming as the nature of the totality and the world we perceive with our senses and instruments as abstractions or projections from the totality. He views the puzzling behaviors of matter at the quantum level and the mysteries of consciousness interacting with matter as artifacts of universal laws in the totality or implicate state that are projected into realms we can observe in the explicate state. He believes it is unlikely that we will ever be able to discover those universal laws.

10

Advaita Vedanta

ADVAITA VEDANTA IS a particular Hindu form of nondual
philosophy. Vedanta refers to the study and tradition of the
wisdom of the Hindu scriptures including the Vedas, Upanishads, and Bhagavad Gita. Advaita means "not-two" and
refers to the belief that Atman (the essence of the self) and
Brahman (the essence of divinity) are one. It is epitomized in
the saying *Tat twam asi,* "Thou art that," from the *Chandogya
Upanishad.* In this passage, the sage Uddalaka is instructing
his son Svetaketu:

> "Bring me a fruit from this banyan tree."
> "Here it is, father."
> "Break it."
> "It is broken, Sir."
> "What do you see in it?"
> "Very small seeds, Sir."
> "Break one of them, my son."
> "It is broken, Sir."
> "What do you see in it?"
> "Nothing at all, Sir."

> Then his father spoke to him: "My son, from the
> very essence in the seed which you cannot see comes in
> truth this vast banyan tree.

Believe me, my son, an invisible and subtle essence
is the Spirit of the whole universe. That is Reality. That
is Atman. Thou art that."[1]

The passage continues with more examples of the subtle essence in things and repetition of the phrase "Thou art that."

Shankaracharya

Though Advaita Vedanta dates to an earlier time, it was
systematized into a comprehensive philosophy in the eighth
century CE by Shankaracharya. His work had a major influence on the direction of Hinduism and helped to restore its
dominance in India when Buddhism was gaining popularity.

In Advaita Vedanta, the absolute is called Brahman. The
nature of Brahman is perfect intelligence. It is eternal, cause-
less, omniscient, omnipotent, and all-pervading. Brahman is
entirely transcendent. It is pure potentiality or all possibility. Although many descriptions hint at its nature, it is indescribable, ineffable. The traditional way to approach an
understanding of it is *neti, neti,* (not this, not that). All one can
say about it is what it is not. In Advaita Vedanta, however,
its ineffability does not mean that it is empty or the void as
Buddhism concludes. Any description would only limit what
is unlimited.

Brahman is understood to be the source of the immanent
world of objects through emanation. As the source of apparent fullness, Brahman cannot be an empty void. It is characterized by *satchitananda, sat* being pure existence, *chit* being
consciousness or pure intelligence, and *ananda* being bliss or
perfect happiness and peace. Though Brahman cannot be
understood by the dualistic mind that can only know things

1. *The Upanishads*, trans. Juan Mascaro (Baltimore, MD: Penguin Books, 1973),
117.

by contrast and comparison, unity consciousness can be experienced directly. For those who have loved know what love is, the experience of love can't be explained to someone who has not known it. It can be described, but the experience is beyond any description. Those who have experienced oneness by losing the sense of duality explain their experience as well as they can as satchitananda.

What is Atman? Amid the changeable components of our identity—body, mind, heart, and personality—there is a capacity to observe what is happening that is detached and objective. It remains unchanged through life. If body and mind are the objects of our perception of ourselves, then the subject is this witnessing faculty. The witness is what Shankaracharya calls the Atman. A tenet of Advaita Vedanta conveys that Atman and Brahman are the same. When one is witnessing one's life, one could imagine that our experience of witnessing is Brahman peering through our eyes. Then the same Brahman is witnessing through the eyes of every person. We could generalize further, saying that Brahman looks through the eyes of every living being that has eyes. Thus, we conclude that every instance of consciousness in nature finds its ground in the *chit* or pure intelligence of Brahman.

The equivalence of Brahman and Atman raises difficult questions. How does transcendence generate immanence? Is pure consciousness degraded from its original state when it is threaded into human consciousness? Does looking through human eyes change the consciousness of Brahman? How does the seamless One become divided into the existence of multiple beings? If the one cause is self-sufficient, why does it produce such a multitude of effects? Is the One the only reality and the many unreal?

Shankaracharya answers that there is one Cause independent of all effects while every effect depends on the Cause. In the realm of being, only the One is real in the sense that it is unchanging and persistent. In contrast, the many have existence temporarily and then lose it. There is a continual flux in the world of the many. It is the world of becoming. As it unfolds, it is continually being born, reaching fullness, and dying to make way for the next wave. It is not real in its aspect of being as it is temporary, fleeting, always passing away. Yet, in another sense, it is real and not illusory. It is truly there. Samuel Johnson's answer to idealism, the notion that matter is only a projection of imagination, was to give its proponent a kick in the shin. We certainly experience the material world as real to our senses.

Shankaracharya sees the effect of the Cause not as the creation of an object out of nothing. Rather, he describes becoming as a process in which a pattern emerges that was already latent as essence. When it emerges, it is given a name and form, but it is not entirely new. For example, when a pot is created from clay, the pot now has a name and a form, but it is still clay. A seed is another example of an essence that contains in latency a tree with its branches, leaves, flowers, and fruit. The nature of the Cause is that it is the depository of all essences. All effects are distinguished from a common ground by giving them a name and form.

If Atman is Brahman—if our essential self as witness is the same as the One Self—why is the true reality hidden from our eyes? Why do we see only the transient world? For Shankaracharya, the reason is that we are blinded by *avidya*, or ignorance. Avidya arises from two sources, the restlessness of the mind and the insecurity of the ego. Our mind is preoccupied by the drama and endless novelty of the world. As a result, it resists coming to stillness. If it could come to rest, the curtain would be drawn revealing an inner truth that is staring us in the face but always missed.

Ego also grips us by its rapacious needs. We need to feel loved, understood, accepted. Our perceived separateness makes us feel lonely. We can never stack up against our inherent sense of values, so we judge ourselves and feel unworthy.

Our natural drives become distorted as greed, lust, and self-absorption. The result of monkey mind and self-absorption is ignorance of the truth.

Avidya on the personal level corresponds to *maya* in the collective consciousness. Originally, maya is the artistry of Brahman, the aesthetic imagination that paints the picture of the world. However, maya gets distorted into a private world by the individual ego anxious to protect its presumed primacy. Maya is typically understood as the illusion of a world of separate objects and beings. However, for those who have glimpsed the truth of underlying oneness, maya is a vision of love, harmony, and beauty continually emanating from Brahman. To imagine that Brahman would have a purpose in emanating the world of maya would be to limit the immeasurable Brahman. Shankaracharya surmises that the world of maya has no purpose that we can understand. Rather he calls it *leela*, the play of Brahman.

If avidya typically blocks the Atman from recognizing itself and the truth of oneness, where does the knowledge of Brahman come from? The knowledge of Brahman comes from the wisdom of the Upanishads and Vedas. To achieve this knowledge, sages had to find ways to discipline the mind through concentration and meditation and to overcome a false identification with the ego. Shankaracharya advocates the path of devotion to an ideal image of God as a way to withdraw attention from the demands of the ego. As a believer in the nondual Brahman, beyond any attributes, he justifies his practice of worshipping a personal God of many attributes as a natural reaction to a beautiful emanation of maya. He took Ishwara, a name for Shiva, the God he worshipped, to be as real as the material world, another aspect of Creation.

If one follows the path of mental discipline and sincere worship or other paths that address the confusion of avidya, one can arrive at *brahmanubhava*, a direct experience of Brahman, or oneness with all. It is reported to be an experience of peace and bliss. One's view of reality is transformed. One sees everything as interconnected. The drama of what is passing seems unreal. One is freed from the narrowness and agitation of the ego.

Ramana Maharshi

In the first half of the twentieth century, Ramana Maharshi was perhaps the most well-known practitioner and teacher of Advaita Vedanta. As a child in a religious Indian family, he was fascinated by stories he read about illuminated souls associated with a legendary temple devoted to Shiva. He had a natural gift for inner inquiry and deep absorption. At the age of sixteen, he was overcome with a feeling of immanent death. Lying on the floor, he asked himself who was dying. The answer came that his body was dying, but something would continue to live. That something felt like a current inside him. He identified that current as Shiva. At that moment, his personal identity died. It was replaced by an identification with the One current that flows through everything.

He tried to continue to live a normal life, but was continually pulled into inward absorption. After a few months, he decided to leave home and go to the Shiva temple he had read about. When he arrived, he went into a silent inner absorption that lasted three years. During that time, he didn't speak, paid no attention to his body, and only ate when others force-fed him. Gradually, a small community gathered around him. At first, he ran away from others who came seeking help, but when he couldn't avoid them, he concluded that it was his mission to offer what he could. Later in life, he became active at his ashram, involved in the design and construction of buildings, and met with groups or individuals whenever they presented themselves. His teaching was offered mainly through silent presence.

Though he was deeply devoted to Shiva in the form of the temple of Arunachala, Ramana Maharshi taught mainly about what Shankaracharya called brahmanubhava, awakening to the oneness of being. His method is called self-inquiry and he is known for his oft-repeated question, "Who am I?" He discouraged answers such as "I am consciousness," because such answers are conceptions. Rather, he urged devotees to seek the experience at the root of the question. What is the "I" that gives rise to our feeling of existence? What does one find at the root of Being? He regarded the mind as a misleading renegade that keeps us away from the discovery of our true nature.

As a telling metaphor, Ramana Maharshi used the example of a bull that is kept in a pen. When the pen door is opened, the bull wanders out in search of food. Not knowing about human boundaries, the bull seeks food in the fields of neighbors who drive it away with sticks and stones. Yet, it keeps returning to the fields, driven by its desire for food. The bull in this metaphor is the mind living in the pen of the heart. Yogic exercises seek to contain the bull of the mind. This only works for a period of time, because the mind still has the desire to wander. Ramana's method is to draw the bull of the mind back into the pen by offering it fresh grass. The doors of the pen remain open. The bull continues to wander. Eventually, it realizes there is always a supply of food available in the pen, and stops wandering.

There is a further step in which the bull is killed. In a sense, the mind has to be killed. One might instead say that the Self absorbs the mind when the mind stops wandering. What dies is the mind's sense of being a separate independent self. One can give one's mind its freedom by leaving the pen door open, and attract the mind back into the pen by seeking the sweetness and peace of a true intimation of the

Self, by asking, "Who am I?" Yet, only the Self can reabsorb the mind. There is no technique to do this for oneself. That step in the West is called grace.

Bohm is concerned with movement and the unfoldment of becoming. Ramana Maharshi stresses the realization of Being as the true and only Self. Yet, perhaps the seeming difference in their viewpoints is only semantic. Ramana Maharshi described his awakening experience as a current or flow. Bohm imagined essence as an implicate state, a state of the ceaseless flowing of the holomovement.

Ken Wilber's Summary

Ken Wilber has written extensively about nondual philosophy in many of his books. His writings on the subject are collected in *The Simple Feeling of Being*.[2]

Wilber begins with the key question posed by Ramana Maharshi, "Who am I?" Who is it that is conscious of the environment, of other beings, of myself? It can't be my body, thoughts, or feelings because I am conscious of them. There is in me a witness that observes whatever I am aware of. That witness is pure subject. It is not an object. There is no way to witness the witness. And I am that witness.

He describes how one can go further. One can witness the ego as a self-contraction. It is a subtle contraction by which we unconsciously hold ourselves together. The ego is not an object, it is an effort. We can't do away with the ego through effort, because we would then be engaged in two efforts, one conscious and the other unconscious. Instead, we can simply witness the self-contraction without judgment. By holding this contraction in awareness without any attempt to change it, we have already begun to free ourselves from its grip. Wilber calls the experience of oneness One Taste.

2. Ken Wilber, *The Simple Feeling of Being* (Boston: Shambhala, 2004).

In that simple, easy, effortless state—while you are not trying to get rid of the self-contraction but simply feeling it—and while you are therefore resting as the great Witness or Emptiness that you are—One Taste might more easily flash forth. There is nothing that you can do to bring about (or cause) One Taste—it is always already fully present, it is not the result of temporal actions, and you have never lost it anyway.[3]

Identifying with being the witness gives one a feeling of freedom and expansiveness. I am awareness and the body is an object in my awareness. Whatever I observe is in my awareness. Ordinarily, we think of ourselves as in the body, which is in the environment, which is in the universe. Being the witness, the body, the environment, and the universe are all in me. The witness is not an object, so we can't tie it down to a location in space. It is not located somewhere in the brain. As the witness is pure subject, location in space is inside awareness, but awareness itself can't be located.

Dzogchen is a Tibetan Buddhist form of nondual philosophy. Wilber provides an explanation of its essence. Since Spirit[4] is all-pervading, there is no place it is not. Therefore, it is present in your awareness right now. What's more, you don't need to be "enlightened" to be aware of it. As spirit as a level of reality is already present, you are aware of it every moment. Enlightenment is not something that will happen in the future. Enlightenment can't have a beginning or an end. It is always present. Dzogchen doesn't recommend meditation as a way to find spirit. Meditation as a way to change one's consciousness is not needed. No change is needed. Rather, what Dzogchen offers is what is called "the pointing

---

3. Ibid., 22.

4. Wilber uses "spirit" to mean the highest level of reality and "Spirit" to mean the ground of reality inclusive of all levels. Ken Wilber, *Quantum Questions: Mystical Writings of the World's Greatest Physicists* (Boston: Shambhala, 2001), 16.

out instructions." The teacher helps the student recognize what is already there.

> Thus, according to these traditions, basic awareness is not hard to reach, it's impossible to avoid, and the so-called "paths" to the Self are really obstacle courses.[5]

The awareness that the Dzogchen teacher points to is nothing special. It is simple but subtle and hard to see. Wilber writes that once one sees it, it is obvious. Whatever one's state of consciousness is, that's it. It is always there. The way to recognize it is to stop trying. Seeking it gets in the way. Relaxation and surrender to the direct experience of witnessing helps one see it. When one sees it, one is transformed.

> So you won't see anything in particular. Whatever is arising is fine. Clouds float by in the sky, feelings float by in the body, thoughts float by in the mind—and you can effortlessly witness all of them. They all spontaneously arise in your own present, easy, effortless awareness. And this witnessing awareness is not itself anything specific you can see. It is just a vast background sense of Freedom—or *pure Emptiness*—and in that pure Emptiness, which you are, the entire manifest world arises. You are that Freedom, Openness, Emptiness—and not any itty bitty thing that arises in it.[6]

Awareness as a state of being can't be pinned down. It is pure and contentless, though it is capable of containing anything and everything. It is always there. We take it for granted. We identify ourselves as aware beings, but usually that is one aspect of our identity. With the pointing out instructions, the Dzogchen teacher helps students recognize that the

5. Wilber, *Simple Feeling*, 137–38.
6. Ibid.,18–19.

essence of one's identity is pure subject. But "subject" is only a name. The direct experience has no name.

> No objects, no subjects, only this. No entering this state, no leaving it; it is absolutely and eternally and always already the case: the simple feeling of being, the basic and simple immediacy of any and all states, prior to the four quadrants [Wilber's four aspects of experience], prior to the split between inside and outside, prior to seer and seen, prior to the rise of worlds, ever-present as pure Presence, the simple feeling of being: empty awareness as the opening or clearing in which all worlds arise, ceaselessly: I-I is the box the universe comes in.[7]

Wilber uses Ramana Maharshi's term "I-I." It refers to two aspects of what is called the bare experience of "I." When we arrive at the bare experience of "I" by disidentifying with body, mind, feelings, and personality, we first sense it as personal essence. Then, we discover that the "I" we encounter is universal. By using the symbol "I-I," Ramana Maharshi suggests that the universal and personal are two facets of one awareness.

Wilber also uses the term "always already" to suggest both the immediacy of the direct encounter with awareness and its givenness, that is, it has always been and will always be. He also identifies the simple feeling of being as Presence.

> This unwavering Presence is not entered. There is no stepping into it or falling out of it. . . . It is absolutely not an experience—not an experience of momentary states, not an experience of self, not an experience of no-self, not an experience of relaxing, not an experience of surrendering: it is the Empty opening or clearing in which all of those experiences come and go, an

7. Ibid., 184.

opening or clearing that, were it not always already Present, no experiences could arise in the first place.

This pure Presence is not a change of state, not an altered state, not a different state, not a state of peace or calm or bliss (or anger or fear or envy). It is the simple, pure, immediate, present awareness in which all of those states come and go, the opening or clearing in which they arise, remain, pass; arise, remain, pass . . .

And yet there is something that does not arise or remain or pass—the simple opening, the immediateness of awareness, the simple feeling of Being.[8]

Here, we are thrown back on the inadequacy of dualistic language and thinking. No one can grasp common experiences like the taste of food or the scent of flowers simply from a description. Subtle aspects of those experiences can be described that sharpen one's sense of discrimination but only after one has "tasted" by having a direct nonverbal experience. This is why Wilber calls the direct experience of the state of oneness One Taste.

> It is extremely difficult to adequately discuss no-boundary awareness or non-dual consciousness. This is because our language—the medium in which all verbal discussion must float—is a language of boundaries. . . . Even to say "reality is no-boundary awareness" is still to create a distinction between boundaries and no-boundary! . . . That "reality is no-boundary" is true enough, provided we remember that no-boundary awareness is a direct, immediate, and nonverbal awareness, and not a mere philosophical theory. It is for these reasons that the mystic-sages stress that reality lies beyond names and forms, words and thoughts, divisions and boundaries.[9]

8. Ibid., 220.
9. Ibid., 182–83.

Is God the Nondual?

Across the world, in many cultures, over millennia, humanity has felt the need to worship. Scientific skepticism has attributed this universal desire to a superstitious fear of the unknown, to a hope that prayer and sacrifice would propitiate supernatural forces and bring about a measure of security. In contemporary times, scientists say that empirical knowledge has replaced superstition with an understanding of natural forces and now it is time to outgrow primitive beliefs. Scientific understanding is built upon rational inquiry and logical deduction. But what of the understanding of the heart? We began part 3 by noting that as the heart opens, we are able to come closer to others and go beyond dualistic thinking. As the heart opens, we are drawn to each other, and our ideals become more meaningful. Another form of knowing opens. We are able to gain deeper understanding through intuition.

We may think of the shamans of ancient cultures as medicine men or magicians. What if they were mystic sages gifted with the ability to enter deep states of meditation and experience brahmanubhava, a direct experience of the One? The sages in the Hindu tradition produced the source material for Advaita Vedanta, the Vedas and Upanishads. The prophets of the Abrahamic religions were also mystic sages. Their brahamanubhava or exalted states resulted in revelations about the nature of reality and truth and are recorded in the world's scriptures. This reflects a different view of the origin of religions. Rather than superstitious propitiation, hasn't religion emerged from the revelatory experience of illuminated souls?

What is the meaning of God as nondual reality? How do we relate to such a notion of God? Use of the word "God" implies a feeling of sacredness or awe. This is the feeling reported by mystics who have had a direct experience of the One. For most of us who haven't had that experience, we can have a vicarious experience in the presence of a sage. For example, visitors to Ramana Maharshi's ashram reported feeling a sacred atmosphere in his presence.

Familiar conceptions of God are interpreted by the dualistic mind. Martin Buber recognized ways of relating to God expressed as I-It and I-Thou. Scientific atheists who deny the existence of a personal God might relate to God as I-It attesting to the mystery and awesomeness of nature. The I-Thou relationship acknowledges the knowledge and seeking of the heart. Going beyond the dualistic nature of the I-Thou relationship, the nondual vision of God, in the language of Ramana Maharshi, is expressed as "I-I." Our individual sense of "I" as the essence of our being is in relationship to the primal "I." That relationship is not dual. There are not two "I"s. The "I" that seems to be separate and independent is an illusion. The nature of the relationship with a nondual God is absorption into the One.

Ideas about a personal or impersonal God no longer apply. These terms only have meaning as long as we view God from the perspective of an individual self. If the personal self is understood as a mirage, we have to shift to the point of view of the one and only Self. That view is no longer an imagined perspective. Ibn 'Arabi would say, God knows God's Self through the knowledge God gains of God's Self through our knowledge of God. In this conception, God is the essence of everything, and we are instruments affording unique ways in which God comes to know God's Self.

The near-universal inclination to worship the divine can then be understood as an activity of the Only Being, inspired and uplifted by the continual revelation of its own countenance.

God as the One is a beautiful concept, but it is not accessible to most as a convincing experience. While we can admire nondual philosophy for its depth and promise, we might also wonder what meaning it holds for our everyday lives. We function in a dualistic consciousness. In this age of the dominance of scientific skepticism, how can we understand God in our daily lives? This is the subject of part 4.

Part 4

A Stepping-Stone

11

Create God for Yourself

We see in the words of philosophers, mystics, sages, thinkers, and of prophets a great importance given to self-realization. But if I were to explain about self-realization, I should say the first step to self- realization is God-realization. The one who realizes God in the end realizes self. But the one who realizes self, he never realizes God. And that is the difficulty today with those who search after spiritual truth intellectually. They read many books about occultism, and about esotericism, and mysticism, and they find self-realization most emphasized. And therefore they think that what they have to do in the world is to come to that self-realization. And they think it is just as well to omit God. God in reality is the key to the spiritual perfection; God is the stepping-stone to the self-realization. God is the way which covers the knowledge of the whole being. And if God is omitted, then nothing is reached.

—Hazrat Inayat Khan, "Stages on the Path
of Realization," *Complete Works*, 1926 II

PART 3 CONCLUDED with a recognition of the powerful state of brahmanubhava, absorption in the One. If one sets out to gain a deeper appreciation of reality by going beyond dualistic thinking, one may achieve an intellectual understanding of truth, but what will one gain from it? Intellectual pursuit is not enough to reach brahmanubhava. Hazrat Inayat Khan points out that intellectuals such as scientists and

philosophers who try to swallow nondual philosophy will suffer indigestion.

> They are the people who have eaten of the truth with-
> out digesting it. It is like swallowing pebbles, which one
> can never digest. They have some part of the truth, but
> they do not profit by it.[1]

Knowledge gained by opening the heart requires trust.
When we open our hearts in relationship to others, we risk
being disappointed or rejected. Some religions have depict-
ed God as intimidating, as we explored in the story of Job,
in which God overwhelms Job's plaintive questions by sheer
majesty of Being. Jelaluddin Rumi tells the story of a gnat
that brings a complaint against the West Wind to the court
of Solomon. Solomon listens to the gnat's grievances, then
calls for testimony from the West Wind. When the West
Wind arrives, the gnat is swept away.

Are we no more than a gnat before the mighty West Wind
of God? How can we have a trusting relationship with something so awesome? Though God may be awesome, God remains invisible to our senses and our inquiring mind. Why
should we believe such a thing as God exists? As a Muslim
youth, Hazrat Inayat Khan made the radical decision to stop
repeating the prescribed prayers five times a day. He boldly
told his grandfather, Maulabakhsh, a famous Indian musi-
cian, about his decision.

> One evening in the summer time I was kneeling on the
> house-roof, offering my Namaz (prayers) to Allah the
> Great, when the thought smote me that although I had
> been praying so long with all trust, devotion, and hu-
> mility, no revelation had been vouchsafed to me, and

---

1. Hazrat Inayat Khan, "The God Ideal," in *The Unity of Religious Ideals*, vol. IX,
The Sufi Message of Hazrat Inayat Khan (London: Barrie and Rockliff, 1963), 89.

that it was therefore not wise to worship Him, that One whom I had neither seen nor fathomed. I went to my grandfather and told him I would not offer any more prayers to Allah until I had both beheld and gauged Him. "There is no sense in following a belief and doing as one's ancestors did before one, without knowing the true reason," I said.

Instead of being vexed Maulabakhsh was pleased with my inquisitiveness, and after a little silence he answered me by quoting a sura of the Quran, "We will show them our signs in the world and in themselves, that the truth may be manifested to them." And then he soothed my impatience and explained, saying, "The signs of God are seen in the world, and the world is seen in thyself."[2]

Young Inayat Khan was frustrated with the lack of any visible evidence of God. Quoting from the Qur'an, his grandfather suggested a different approach. If what you are told about God doesn't make God real for you, then create God for yourself. God is created through the imagination. Look for God not in the abstract, in the heavens, in the transcendent, but let your imagination work on God the Immanent. Find God in nature, in your relationships with others, and in your inner feelings. Maulabakhsh described a path designed to open the heart rather than perplex the mind. What we find in nature, in family and friends, and in our self is beauty. By opening the heart we find beauty, and by finding beauty we open the heart.

What one finds in the heart is a capacity to love. Love is the magic element. Love opens the imagination to appreciate, to be thankful. The more the heart opens, the more

2. Hazrat Inayat Khan, "Confessions," in *The Vision of God and Man; Confessions; Four Plays*, vol. XII, *The Sufi Message of Hazrat Inayat Khan* (London: Barrie and Rockliff, 1967), 130–31.

beauty one can perceive. This is what happens when one falls in love with another. It is as though a threshold is crossed and appreciation changes into idealization. The beauty one has glimpsed turns golden. We are familiar with how this can happen with a beloved partner. We become fascinated with the person. We want to be in that person's presence all the time. This transformation can happen suddenly or gradually over time.

These experiences can also happen with the God we create in our imagination. If we seek and appreciate beauty in nature, for example, our capacity for appreciation grows. As we focus increasingly on beauty, our appreciation may expand so much that we cross a threshold beyond which the beauty becomes dazzling. We feel an intimacy with our environment, we feel at home. We want to remain in that state. We fall in love with the presence of God in nature. This is the experience of communion with nature, and with God in nature. We can find communion with God in a circle of friends, in a loving relationship, and in the peace and silence we find when we are at rest in our self. This is not a theoretical God, not merely a concept of God, but a presence.

In Advaita Vedanta philosophy, the divine is the nondual, the Only Being. Vedanta has sometimes been called atheism because it does away with a personal God. Yet, Shankaracharya was an ardent worshipper of Ishwara or Shiva. He also worshipped the divine in feminine form as Devi. Ramana Maharshi was also dedicated to Shiva and regularly participated in rituals of worship. Although Shankaracharya and Ramana Maharshi were illuminated souls who had realized the One in all, they still felt a need and desire to worship a personal God.

Shankaracharya had a keen mind. He was able to prevail in most of his debates with rival Indian scholars. Through precision, consistency, and comprehensiveness, he gave Advaita Vedanta philosophy a firm foundation. Ramana Maharshi had an inherent gift for focused inquiry. No matter what he was going through, he could dispassionately examine his experience and gain deep insights. Both souls had extreme mental gifts. It appears that they found balance and relief for the mind by diving into feelings of devotion. Their devotional life ensured that insights of the mind would be given life and fire by engaging love in the heart.

The God Ideal

How does one go about creating a God to believe in? One may have absorbed ideas about God from a religious upbringing. Religious ideas about God come from the holy scriptures, an expression of the experience of prophetic revelation. Such beliefs may have been influenced by cultural context. One may have had influential people in one's life who have conveyed their beliefs or transmitted an impression of what is holy by their personality and behavior. As one matures and becomes more independent, one may sort out from beliefs handed down, those that impress and inspire from those one questions.

On what basis does one do this sorting? Each of us is a unique collection of sensitivities. For some, the impression of the senses is inspiring. The beauty of nature with its constantly changing tableaux, the play of colors in the environment, the intricacy of design, and the fascinating ways of living creatures may lift one's spirit. For another, the charm of personality and the emotional fulfillment of relationship could be what one prizes in life. Yet another might be fascinated with the way things work, the intricacies of nature's phenomena, and the capacity of the human mind to perceive the secrets of its order. Each of us has a unique code of values, what we find most important and meaningful. What inspires us, what we hold most dear, is the ultimate criterion on which we build our beliefs.

One begins by sorting through inherited beliefs to find those that match what one inherently values. One can then actively build on those beliefs by seeking out and appreciating what one values. The lover of nature, for example, can look for the spirit that infuses nature with its beauty and harmony.

If one looks at a tree, one first sees the surface of the tree, the trunk covered with bark, the branches, and leaves. It is not only the surface design of the tree that pleases. The tree has a life energy that is apparent over the seasons as it grows larger, producing twigs, branches, leaves, and possibly flowers. If one knows about the tree's biology, one may be aware of the roots drawing nutrients from the soil, of veins running up the trunk that deliver food to the branches and leaves, of leaves drinking in sunlight and producing chlorophyll.

One might develop a relationship with the tree as a living organism, perhaps recognizing shared traits or qualities. Through imagination, one can discover a living essence, the source of the tree's beautiful qualities. One can similarly develop a belief in a living God, an essence present in all things that is the source of their beauty. Such a belief is not only of the mind. One's love imbues it with a vital presence. It is something one can feel, something comforting and uplifting. It is the spirit of the Friend.

What is your ideal? What do you value in life? Who are your heroes? If there is an inspiring person in your life or an historical figure you admire, this is a good starting point. Every person is limited, with some flaw, even those we consider ideal souls. Starting from a limited personality, one can use one's imagination to supply whatever is missing to create for oneself an ideal personality. If the person one chooses exemplifies one's ideal of compassion, as an artist of the imagination one can envision that person as embodying even greater compassion. Continuing one's efforts, embellishing the image until it sparkles with the perfection of compassion, one will have taken the next step. Whatever qualities appeal to one's innate values, when one can evoke them in a state of perfection, clothed in a personality, one has made for oneself a guiding star, a model for one's life.

If one has done this with an open and loving heart, then one is drawn to this ideal, one can have communion with one's ideal. The more one remembers it, the more it becomes a presence. One can feel its influence in one's life. The presence of the Friend—like the presence of a human friend—brings comfort, security, peace, happiness, and confidence.

Belief

What is the origin of belief? Every child is a born believer. It readily absorbs what it learns from its parents. The child trusts the knowledge conveyed by the parents. As it grows, if introduced to the religious beliefs of the parents, it trusts this knowledge in the same way. If the parents have no religious beliefs, the child may be influenced by another family member, often a grandmother, or by friends, neighbors, its culture or community.

As the child's mind ripens, it may again be influenced by a powerful figure, a teacher, a preacher, or a philosopher. As a youth, one continues to take in impressions and to question. Yet in youth, one feels a need for independence, and so may test a succession of beliefs by the process of reasoning. If one keeps an open mind, one may be prepared to grow in one's belief. Yet, it is more likely that as one ages, one's beliefs become fixed. One may feel that one has found a comfortable place in a community that shares a belief. Or, one may feel that one has sufficiently examined a range of beliefs and is now satisfied to believe there is nothing beyond humanity to believe in.

For a mystic, belief continues to develop beyond reasoning through experience. There are experiences, mystics would say, that sweep away doubt. Belief then becomes conviction. Skeptics might say that although hallucinogenic experiences can be convincing, to an objective observer, they are clearly projections of the imagination. One can, however, discriminate between hallucinations and mystical experiences. The first is generally dysfunctional and tends to diminish the qualities of the personality, diminish the well-being of the personality, while the second is life changing and transforms the personality in observable and positive ways.

If one cultivates one's ideal with an open heart and mind, one's belief will depend on one's experience. One needn't try to believe in anything. Belief, when it arrives, must arrive naturally. Through the power of will and imagination, one can cultivate from one's internal resources something lying dormant in one's being. When what has been hidden begins to emerge, the experience is out of one's hands. Through one's effort one has awakened it. Although the knowledge that is revealed may not make sense to the mind, the sense it makes to the heart may be much more satisfying.

> It must be remembered that belief is a step on the ladder. Belief is the means and not the end. It leads to realization, and it is not that we come to a belief. And if a man's foot is nailed on the ladder, that is not the object. The object is that he must step on the ladder and climb upwards. If he stands on the ladder, he defeats the objects with which he journeys on the spiritual path.[3]

---

3. Inayat Khan, "Stages on the Path of Self-Realization," *Complete Works of Pir-O-Murshid Hazrat Inayat Khan*, 1926 II, (New Lebanon, NY: Omega Publications, 2011), 304.

12

I Was a Hidden Treasure

SUFI MYSTICS HAVE been deeply impressed by a Hadith Qud-si, a saying of Prophet Muhammad attributed to God speaking, "I was a Hidden Treasure and longed to be known, so I created the World that I might be known." What are the implications of this saying for our relationship to the divine and our reason for existence?

Imagine that at the beginning of time, there is only undifferentiated existence with a capacity for perfect intelligence. There is no content for the intelligence to absorb, so in effect, we could say it is asleep. Consider this parable about how perfect intelligence awakened:

Shimmering intelligence, a seamless ocean of subtle vibration, stirs in its sleep. Intelligence feels the urge to pull itself together and awaken, although as yet it has no inkling of being a self. At first, intelligence is aware only of gentle waves of vibration as a bath of unadorned existence. Intelligence marvels that there is such a thing as existence. In a moment, intelligence becomes aware of being the primal self. The primal self feels that "I" exist. It wonders: What is this mystery of "I"? The primal self realizes that the mystery has something to do with the experience of centering and becoming a witnessing subject.

Now it discovers that besides the mysterious capacity of self, it also has the capacity to learn and to know. The primal self realizes: I know I exist. Soon another subtle capacity stirs. It can explore and seek to know. It feels: I have agency, I have the capacity to act.

The primal self wonders: Why should I act? What motivates me to seek further knowledge? The answer that comes is curiosity. And what is behind curiosity muses the primal self? The answer comes as an echo of the question: the desire to know something else. Yet another subtle capacity of intelligence has awakened, a very important capacity, desire. The primal self asks: Where does that desire come from? And the answer comes from a mysterious well of feeling we call love. Probing deeper, the primal self asks: Where does love come from? It realizes that love is an inherent capacity, as fundamental as existence or intelligence itself. In fact, love, intelligence, and existence all come from the same well. They are different facets of a single gem.

Now that love has awakened, the ears and eyes of the primal self are opened. What do they see? The shimmering ocean of existence, at first apparently uniform, then drawn into a center as the primal self, now begins to unveil itself. In modesty, the ocean of existence reveals only a subtle glimpse of its matchless beauty. From pure subject, the first object is drawn out. A taste of the object's beauty quickens the primal self's flame of desire. It longs to know more intimately the object of its love. The primal self recognizes that what it loves is not separate from itself. How to know better that beauty that is mostly veiled—the Hidden Treasure? The primal self realizes that it must exercise a further subtle capacity that now awakens. It discovers: I have the capacity to express all that is in me. It remembers that it has only to say "Be," and the world of possibilities manifests. Its desire is to articulate itself in a multitude of ways. Witnessing the inherent beauty of its nature fulfills the desire that brought about creation.

Let's follow this story line a little further. The world is the theater of the Self expressing its Hidden Treasure of qualities. When we witness something we consider to be beautiful, there is an intellectual aspect to our appreciation. But what moves or thrills us may be expressed simply as a heartfelt sigh. It is a direct knowing of rightness, of something that stirs us. It uplifts and exalts us. What the Self communicates in each expression of itself fulfills the primal desire to know itself. From the nondual point of view, the Self looking through our eyes satisfies its desire when we appreciate beauty, which is the Self expressed in its many forms. Every object in the world has its share of the Hidden Treasure to express. Every person has a unique gift, a particular combination of beautiful qualities, lying dormant until they find their way to expression.

How do we learn about the qualities we are meant to express, namely, our gift? We know those qualities by paying attention to what moves us or inspires us. Our hidden qualities resonate with those qualities in nature or in another person that we value. What we value becomes the basis of our cultivation of a God ideal, how we create for ourselves our vision or concept of God. To try to create one's self in the image of our values or gifts is like pulling oneself up by one's bootstraps. Instead of trying to mold ourselves into an expression of our gifts, we project before us a vision of the perfection of our ideals. We develop a relationship with that model of what we are meant to be. By infusing our concept of God with all the beauty our imagination can conjure, we withdraw attention from our limited notion of ourself. We begin to let go of our neuroses, worries, and fears. Instead, our attention is directed toward pleasing our Friend. What would make the God we have created happy? When our Friend becomes a living presence for us, we find pleasure in the pleasure of the universal Friend. Then, by reflection, we begin to mirror what we hold before us. Our vision elicits in us the expression that brings fulfillment to our lives.

Perfection and Limitation

There is nothing in the material world that is perfect. We might think a circle is perfect, that it can't be improved upon. An abstract circle as a mathematical idea is perfect, but circles in nature are never perfect. What about a black hole? Wouldn't it be a perfect sphere? According to Stephen Hawking, the surface of a black hole is fuzzy because space-time at the surface fluctuates wildly due to quantum effects. The most accurately engineered metal spheres used by NASA are almost perfect, yet they also have tiny deviations. Beautiful flowers, if one looks closely, always have some flaw, large or small.

If we think of a beautiful quality in a person, we will always be able to improve upon it with our imagination. In mathematics, given a large number as represented by the letter n, one can always think of a larger number, $n + 1$. If we line up the integers starting with 1, they go on as far as we can imagine. This is the basis for the idea of infinity. Similarly, if we lined people up according to their presumed honesty, the line would continue until it included all existing people. Using our imagination, we could go on indefinitely. Nonetheless, we can say that there is a quality of honesty that can't be improved upon. It doesn't single out a particular person, because in the world there is no perfect person. But there can be a perfect quality of honesty.

As demonstrated, we can imagine a relative scale of honesty. We can also imagine the archetype of honesty that is pure with no taint of imperfection. The honesty we see in any individual is derived from the archetype of honesty as an exemplar. In other words, in every person, we see a reflection of perfect archetypal honesty. When perfect honesty takes on a definite form, it conforms to the medium in which it is expressed. That medium is shaped by a central organizing principle we call a self, an ego, or a nafs. The ego is invested in protecting and promoting itself. By virtue of the experiences that have shaped it, it will limit pure honesty in ways that serve it. The result is relative honesty.

All of our qualities and the qualities of others are reflections of perfect qualities. As the archetypal qualities come into name and form, compromises must be made. Actual forms in the world cannot accommodate perfect qualities. Since the limitations of a quality depend on the influence of the ego, for humans, it is possible for the perfect quality to shine through more fully when the ego is subdued. If the ego is suppressed, it reacts with resentment or hostility, limiting the fullness of the quality even further. In contrast, when the ego is brought under control in a self-respecting person—that is to say, in a way that honors the Self—the ego's interference in the transmission of the archetype is reduced. Jesus referred to this possibility of fully or partially expressing a quality when he said, "Neither do men light a candle and put it under a bushel, but on a candlestick, and it giveth light unto all that are in the house" (Matthew 5:15). For a true mystic, the ego is fully subdued, leaving nothing to block the perfect qualities from coming through. Jesus said about this condition, "Be ye therefore perfect, even as your Father which is in heaven is perfect" (Matthew 5:48).

Separation and Unity

Our everyday experience of being in a body, with an inner life that is hidden from others, like one island in a sea of unbridgeable waters, makes it difficult to believe that reality is seamless oneness. Against loneliness, we seek friendship or romance or the closeness of family. The Sufis say that human beings have a persistent longing that can't be satisfied by any relationship in this life.

What is the intimacy we long for? Closeness to another, feeling at home being oneself with another. We want to know another person, to plumb the mystery, and we want to be known. In ancient times, "to know another" referred to the intimacy of sexual union. In that act, there is a culmination when one's sense of separateness from the other person disappears. During the experience of union, there is a feeling of deep peace, the burdens of everyday life are lifted, and the underlying longing is temporarily satisfied. It is not just a physical hormonal reaction. Psychologically, one has set down one's ego. When the ego is set aside and one feels secure, a feeling of well-being arises.

Mystics wish for unity with the One or the Beloved or the All. They aspire to the goal of setting aside the ego or even of freeing themselves entirely from the ego. They wish to overcome separateness. If separateness is banished, only the Self remains. Wherever you turn, from the mystic's perspective, there is the face of God.

> There is a superlative "I" behind my "I" forever;
> O take away my "I" that so ails me from between
> Thou and me.[1]

While mystics seek this unity, Sufi mystic Ahmad Ghazali perhaps surprisingly claims that God wishes for separation. The true state of the all-pervading intelligence is union and Oneness. However, in the state of Oneness, the One Being is alone. It has no partner with whom to experience relationship and love. This all-pervading intelligence created the world to know itself. The creation was not an intellectual exercise. It was motivated by desire. The fulfillment of that desire comes through loving relationship. Through relationship with human beings, the One fulfills its longing to know itself.

1. Al Hallaj, quoted in Pir Vilayat Inayat Khan, *In Search of the Hidden Treasure* (New York: Jeremy Tarcher/Putnam, 2003), 141.

What is the nature of falling in love? We see in another something we admire. Falling in love is a resonance between two souls. Our admiration opens a window, and we see not just the ordinary human qualities we see in many others but magical amplified qualities. We get a glimpse of the soul of our beloved. What we see is so attractive, so exhilarating, we can't stop thinking about the other person. Our heart opens. We discover the feeling of love that was formerly veiled. Having a living heart is like being born into a new life. We don't want to give it up, and at the same time, we know that loving is dangerous. We can easily be hurt. We want to put a shield over our heart to protect it.

If the purpose of creating the world was so the Hidden Treasure can know itself, the One Being will not be satisfied with a distant aesthetic appreciation. Its nature is love. Therefore, its satisfaction comes from fulfilled relationship. Humans, in their desire for a fulfilled relationship with the divine, seek union. Their fulfillment is in surrendering the tension and distress of limitation and discovering instead the peace and harmony of perfection. From the opposite point of view, the One whose nature is perfection discovers the myriad ways that its true nature can be expressed through limited forms. The One enjoys the flowing of love toward its lover, be that divine, or human, or toward the beauty of the world. Human limitation receives love from the One in the form of *rahman*, infinite compassion, and *rahim*, everlasting mercy.

13

Relationship of God and Human

The Seed of God

IF GOD IS the One nondual seamless reality, what is the relationship of God to the human being? One metaphor says a human being is like a wave in the ocean. Momentarily, a wave has its own form and can be distinguished from the bulk of the ocean. However, a wave is not a separate object. It is a formation of the ocean itself. There is no boundary between the wave and the ocean. Prophet Muhammad said that the soul is an activity of God. Similarly, we could say the wave is an activity of the ocean. The wave has no independent existence. This metaphor describes one aspect of the relationship of God and human beings. It suggests that our life is a natural phenomenon like the rising of a wave. It rises and falls again as have so many waves before us and around us. Do we rise and fall simply because that is the nature of the ocean, or does our activity also have meaning?

In another metaphor, God is described as a seed. In the *Chandogya Upanishad*, the sage Svetaketu asks his son to bring him a piece of fruit from the banyan tree. His son breaks open the fruit and finds very small seeds. Then he breaks open a seed and finds nothing. Svetaketu points out that from this invisible essence comes the giant banyan tree. A seed is simple and may be empty inside. Yet it contains in its essence all that the tree will produce. It has creative power. It contains the plan for the tree in its DNA. Is there an invisible essence in the DNA?

> It is that seed which is the secret of the plant, which is the source and the goal of that plant. It is that seed which was the beginning, it is from out of that seed that the root came, and the seedling came out, and so it became a plant, and then that seed disappeared. But after the coming of the leaves and branches and the flowers it appeared again. It appeared again, not as one seed, but several seeds, in multiplicity, and yet it is the same.[1]

In this metaphor, the original seed is God, and the seed that comes forth from its fruit is the human being. Why is the human not just another part of the plant that grew from the original seed? Because humans have the creative power of thought and this is the secret of the seed. We have the power to create something new through imagination and to then make what was imagined tangible. What is the plant that results from the human as seed? The plant is the outcome of what the human creates consciously or unconsciously. And the great forest that grows from human seeds is a civilization. It has its branches and leaves. It produces fruits of knowledge, art, government, and wisdom. The forest of civilization grows from the collective influence of many human seeds. The original seed expresses itself through the many seeds it produced.

Within a seed, everything that will come out of that seed can be found in potential. In this metaphor, a human

---

1. Hazrat Inayat Khan, "Man, the Seed of God," in *The Complete Works, Original Texts: Lectures on Sufism*, 1923 II (London: East-West Publications, 1988), 791–92.

being, as the seed that comes from the original seed of God, contains in essence everything one sees in the world. If only the qualities of the animals were seen in humans, evolution could be the explanation. However, humans show qualities beyond the inheritance of species. For example, the fruitfulness of trees and vegetables, their ripeness and unripeness, the qualities of flowing or dammed-up water, the hardness of stone, the shininess of metals and gems, the qualities of sun and moon. All these qualities can be found in humans. The moods and character of humans reflect all the qualities of the natural world. This metaphor of the human being as the seed coming out of the plant of the manifested world that grew from the seed of God agrees with the revelation that humans are created in the image of God.

> The man who wishes to understand the relation between man and God, for him the proof of this argument is to be found in everything. And it is this idea which is spoken of in the Bible, in the words where it is said that "In Our Image We have created man." If the seed out of which the plant came, and which came in the result, had said that "Out of my own image I have created the seed which will come forth from the heart of the flower," it would have been the same thing. Only that seed out of which the plant came could have said that "I shall appear in plurality, although in the beginning I am one grain.". . . No doubt, there is some energy, some power, some color, some fragrance in the flower, in the leaf and in the stem; but at the same time all the property that is in the stem, flower, petal and leaves is to be found in the grain.[2]

Hazrat Inayat Khan goes on to show how signs of all aspects of the world can be found in the human being.

2. Ibid., 792.

In this way, the human being has a unique relationship with the seed that is the source of all. Of all creatures, only the human being is seedlike in having the power to create from imagination.

Can we then integrate the notion of one nondual seamless reality with the idea from mystical revelation that the human being is created in the image of God? Suppose we envision the seamless reality as an endless sea of perfect intelligence. As this sea contains within it all possibility, we can imagine it as seedlike. When the impulse comes for the all-pervasive intelligence to draw itself together into a center, its seed nature is triggered into action and the objective world begins to form from the original seed. Matter forms from the condensation of Intelligence. The unitary intelligence begins to objectify itself and turns into consciousness. The plant of the world then grows from the primal seed. When it has transformed from inert matter into the tree of life, finally the seed returns as the human being. It is not the physical appearance of the human that is an image of God. The image is abstract, involving a richness of potential and a capacity to learn, grow, and create.

Are we humans the only culmination of the process of growth from the original seed? This seems unlikely. There may be myriads of seedlike beings scattered throughout the universe. Perhaps one day we will find other seeds like us.

Immanence and Transcendence

"We will show them our signs in the world and in themselves, that the truth may be manifested to them" (Qur'an 41:53). Look for God on the horizons and in oneself. This advice, given to Inayat Khan as a youth by his grandfather, pointed him toward an inquiry into the immanence of God. If God is essence and existence itself, then the divine nature can be seen wherever one looks, not only in the world around one-self but also in the world within. What is one to look for? If one tries to satisfy the mind by finding something tangible, some magical experience or phenomenon, or some subtle discovery, one will be frustrated. How does one find the seed-like nature in oneself that is meant to be an image of God? It is not hard to see one's creativity, or the power of one's imagination. Is that what we are looking for? Where is the sacredness? Where is the awe due to a divine encounter?

There is a door to go through. You can't go through it driven only by a curious mind, as curiosity is too casual here. What is lying in store is too precious to be probed with super-ficial interest. What is to be discovered is meant to be lived, not pigeonholed into a concept or theory.

To prepare oneself, one needs exposure to the transcen-dence of God. Yet, this puts one in a bind. Transcendence is often out of reach from received forms of belief. Religious ideas about God or philosophical viewpoints such as those found in the Advaita Vedanta offer transcendent visions of reality. How does one digest such lofty ideas? They remain as stones in the stomach without the digestive juices that de-pend on appetite.

Imagination carries with it a gift, the ability to conceive of an ideal. Whatever we feed our imagination—a tangible object like a flower, a personality like a hero, or a quality like compassion—we can always imagine a more ideal ver-sion until our imagining exalts us. We then cross a threshold, and our heart wakens to the vision. Objects themselves, even the divine qualities when visible in a person, are limited. By opening the heart, we are able to imagine them in perfection. Seeing them in perfection arouses our admiration. Admiring them further opens our hearts. With an open heart, we are capable of awe. Such love produces a feeling of caring and sacredness.

With an open heart, an appreciation of beauty, and a desire to peer behind the surface in everything, we are ready to pass through the door. Transcendence in the form of concentration on an ideal, on perfection, allows us to see sacredness in nature and in ourselves. It is hidden beneath the surface. It can be seen by those who have eyes and heart to see. Such transcendence prepares us to experience true immanence, the presence of God in ordinary life.

Development, Unfoldment, and Awakening

In ourselves and in nature, we can recognize transcendence and immanence as Being and becoming. Our essential self, our bare sense of I, is a condition of Being. It doesn't change. We recognize, for example, a feeling in ourselves that is the same now as it was in childhood. Our experience of the journey of life, of learning and growing and changing, is a phenomenon of becoming.

David Bohm believed that movement or flow is an essential aspect of nature. He posited a fundamental flow at the root of reality and called it holomovement, indicating that wholeness is inherent in its nature. Becoming is not only a feature of individuals but also of the totality.

Alfred North Whitehead also found becoming to be foundational to his notion of reality. Everything in nature is continually changing. Nothing is absolutely still. From Whitehead's philosophy came process theology, in which even God is considered to be in flux, growing and changing in tandem with nature's evolution and our own growth and change.

In Martin Heidegger's philosophy, not merely attempting to understand what Being is, but striving to live a life of authentic Being is the central focus. He felt that confronting the fear of imminent death is necessary to keep one's attention riveted on what is most important and most needed in life.

Only this degree of alertness can keep one on the track of authenticity. Living an authentic life means living in harmony with Being.

Through the discoveries of modern science, we have become aware of the march of evolution progressing from single-celled species of plants and animals through all the ingenious and aesthetic designs of flora and fauna leading up to the human form. Evolution is a type of becoming as the development of form and capacity. Fundamental capacities such as seeing and hearing have passed through a multitude of variations. The capacities of awareness and responsiveness have also evolved increasingly sophisticated organs for consciousness. From a spiritual point of view, development is a process by which the material of the earth is shaped into an increasingly capacious and sensitive instrument for spirit or universal intelligence. In the language of the mystics, spirit is working its way through dense matter toward a fuller expression of itself.

There is a great deal of potential in us that remains hidden but is available to emerge. What keeps it hidden? The self-concept we have come to own, commonly called ego. Our self-concept is merely a concept. It is who we think we are, but it is provisional. Tomorrow it may change through new experiences. It is a combination of many ideas about our self. It is held together by a sense of self. We hold it not as many separate parts but as a single whole. Compared to the potential we hold inside us the ego is small and narrow. Without the ego, we feel naked, defenseless, empty.

We cling to the ego as we might cling to a tree branch in the dark, not knowing we are only a few inches from the ground beneath. If we could surrender our grip on the flimsy structure that is our ego, we would find solid ground under our feet. As many spiritual teachers have warned, however, this is only true after we have established a healthy ego in the first place. A healthy ego allows an individual form of becoming, a personal evolution, the unfolding of our hidden nature. As we hold our ego more lightly and trust the ground beneath our feet, we open to spirit shining through us. We become more fully who we are by unfolding what is waiting within us to emerge.

Another path of becoming that we all experience to some degree in our lives is the path of realization. The mind opens to wider and wider spaces. As a child, our horizon of under-standing is naive. As a youth, idealism is awakened and we think the world has compromised too much. We protest and rebel and push for more idealistic programs. In adulthood, we assume a burden of responsibilities and feel hemmed in by the demands of practicality. Life may become narrowed to survival. If we are fortunate and have the opportunity to make choices about what we want to do, we often feel limited by our own self-assessment. Life is our teacher. If we take bitter lessons in a constructive way, we come to realizations that gradually free us from the chains we bind ourselves with. There is a truth about our self that is radically different from our usual sense of our self. When we realize that truth, it is as though we had been asleep, and now we are waking up. Awakening in this sense is another form of becoming.

Being is always there. This is why teachers of Dzogchen, a nondual spiritual path, say there is nothing to strive for. We can't reach enlightenment because we are already there and have always been there. We are spiritual beings. Our very existence is itself spirit. It is only our realization of this condition that is lacking. Everything we think and do comes from spirit. Where else could it come from? Our questions and doubts are a process that spirit or Being goes through, a necessary process. We have always been and will always be spirit, unchanging, permanent.

Becoming is triggered by desire. That desire originated in a divine desire as expressed in the Hadith Qudsi quoted earlier: "I was a Hidden Treasure and longed to be known so I created the world in order to be known." We each have an inherent desire to be fully who we are by breaking out of the narrow confines of our ego, unfolding what is hidden in our nature, and seeking perfection in being true to our ideal. In nature, we see the longing of the Hidden Treasure to know itself as the proliferation of forms and capacities. The bounty of "endless forms most beautiful," a comment made by Charles Darwin about his study of nature, is a creative outpouring of aesthetic intelligence reveling in beauty and affection. Longing to know itself, spirit discovers itself in myriad exemplars deriving from archetypal possibilities, and yet it conforms to laws set in motion by its very nature. In its holistic way, nature generates layers upon layers of becoming, building upon accumulated experience. In the human experiment, becoming unfolds primarily on the level of the heart and mind, not only for individuals, but also for communities and the whole of humanity.

Love, Lover, and Beloved

Childhood is a time of self-centeredness and the desire for immediate gratification. To soften their children's demands, parents teach children to share. This lesson often leads to the child's preoccupation with fairness. God forbid that another child should get more than their fair share.

This attitude changes when a youth first experiences infatuation. Respect and caring for the object of one's attraction calls for putting that person first. Love softens the ego. The lover is ready to make sacrifices for the sake of the beloved. The lover idealizes the beloved and wishes to make the beloved happy. Just thinking about the beloved makes the lover happy. The lover may at times forget the worries and self-critical thoughts that otherwise produce unrest.

When the lover is smitten, a window opens. The lover sees something inspiring or moving in the beloved. Though what the lover sees may not be brought into awareness, the qualities observed resonate with the lover's inner sense of self. The lover resonates with the qualities seen in the beloved. This is a kind of awakening in the lover, a discovery of something internal that is meaningful and rewarding. The lover's desire to hold on to that impression of the beloved leads the impression to become a projection of an ideal. However, the beloved is flesh and blood, so disillusion may be waiting in the wings.

This common process of infatuation, of opening the heart, of the ego softening, of becoming preoccupied with the inspiring qualities of the beloved, is a foretaste of what mystics pursue in their spiritual quest. Seeking God on the horizons and in themselves, mystics begin to fall in love, or better yet, to rise in love. They find in nature their ideal of beauty, followed by their ideal of qualities such as compassion, living magnetism, holy presence, and intimacy. As the heart opens, they find these same qualities in themselves. Their egos are softened as they forget to worry about themselves. Their needs and plans seem less important when reality becomes suffused with meaning.

Of course, the ego does not give up so easily. Inherent in the ego is what the Buddha recognized as a grasping urgency. Insecurity is the nature of the ego. In our separateness, we feel so vulnerable, so fragile. Not only are we subject to threats of harm to body and mind, but still worse, our self-worth is precarious. If we come to feel rejected, abandoned, worthless, or unloved, we are vulnerable to despair. When the mystic begins to loosen the bonds of the ego, to undo its frozen grip that clutches for security on anything that promises safety, the ego may respond with despair. A Sufi mystic, Abi'l Khayr, writes,

Let sorrowful longing dwell in your heart,
never give up, never losing hope.
The Beloved says, "The broken ones are My darlings."
Crush your heart, be broken.[3]

Before the ego loses its grip, the mystic may have to go
through disorientation and suffering. Although rationality
can offer a feeling of stability in life, the mystical journey
must go beyond rationality. The sensible reality to which one
has become accustomed may have to be given up. What re-
places rationality or reliance on the mind is faith. Faith is
trust that is rooted in the heart. Trust comes from allowing
oneself to fall, knowing one will be caught. It is an intuitive
knowledge of the heart.

Abi'l Khayr also writes,

If you are seeking closeness to the Beloved,
love everyone.
Whether in their presence or absence,
see only their good.
If you want to be as clear and refreshing as
the breath of the morning breeze,
like the sun, have nothing but warmth and light
for everyone.[4]

As a child, my mother used to tell me, "Look out for number one." In her experience, those with good natures who
trust others are taken advantage of. Abi'l Khayr advises us
to see the ideal in others regardless of their behavior. This
is the ideal one seeks in the horizons and in oneself. One
overlooks the surface of the other person that may not be
to our liking. By truly seeing their underlying goodness, we

3. Shaikh Abu-Saeed Abil-Kheir, *Nobody, Son of Nobody*, renditions by Vraje
Abramian (Prescott, AZ: Holm Press, 2001), 18.
4. Ibid., 33.

may bring it to life. If not, it doesn't mean we are going to be taken advantage of. Seeing the good doesn't mean we will be fooled by the superficial behavior of the other. Seeing the good wherever we look keeps the heart open, cultivates the magical feeling of love, and helps the ego release its insecurity. If good is all around us, at least in the depth of reality, then what can threaten us?

Opening one's heart, one is able to see the beauty everywhere that was hidden by the insecurity of the ego. One's inner qualities are reflected in nature and in others. When the window of the heart opens and one sees one's inspiring qualities outside oneself, the heart comes alive, and one experiences love. One can then project the ideal form of the qualities one admires without fear of disillusionment. One is not projecting the qualities on a fallible human being, but on the essence behind the person or hidden in nature and that essence is as perfect as one can make it.

Hazrat Inayat Khan expresses his experience of the alchemy of love this way:

Wherever I look, I see Thy beloved face, covered under many different veils. The magic power of my ever-seeking eyes lifted the veil from Thy glowing countenance, and Thy smile won my heart a thousand times over. The lustre of Thy piercing glance hath lighted my darkened soul, and now I see the sunshine everywhere.[5]

For the mystic, the happy feeling of infatuation is not temporary. The sunshine one feels when one falls in love becomes a way of life. The inspiring beauty the mystic finds in the Beloved is endless. There is always more to discover. When one has crossed the threshold of intensified feeling,

5. Hazrat Inayat Khan, *Gayan, Vadan, Nirtan* (New Lebanon, NY: Omega Publications, Inc., 2005), 60.

when one's heart has caught fire with love and longing, the
magic of the Beloved's presence is everywhere.

> Every form I see is Thine own form, my Lord,
> And every sound I hear is Thine own voice;
> In the perfume of flowers I perceive the fragrance of
>   Thy spirit;
> In every word spoken to me I hear Thy voice, my
>   Lord.
> All that touches me is Thine own touch;
> In everything I taste I enjoy the savor of Thy delicious
>   spirit.[6]

Seeing the Beloved in the environment and in everyone
one meets, the insecurity of the ego can completely relax and
the grasping for reassurance can be released. The construct
of the ego loses its importance. One can relax into the flow
of spontaneous awareness. Our identity, our sense of self
derives from the primal self, the One Self. As we release our
grip on the anxieties that keep us separate and isolated, we
begin to recover the deeper sense of self, a sense of what
Ken Wilber calls no-boundary consciousness. We recognize
the same essential Self everywhere in the unifying Presence
behind every object. How could we be different from that
all-pervading Presence? The Sufi mystic Mansur al-Hallaj
expresses it this way:

> I am He whom I love,
>   and He whom I love is I:
> We are two spirits
>   dwelling in one body.
> If thou seest me,
>   thou seest Him,

6. Ibid., 103.

And if thou seest Him,
 thou seest us both.[7]

In the words of Hazrat Inayat Khan, the feeling is expressed as a swinging of consciousness between two states.

> When we are face to face, Beloved, I do not know whether to call Thee me, or me Thee! I see myself when Thou art not before me; when I see Thee my self is lost to view. I consider it good fortune when Thou art alone with me, but when I am not there at all, I think it the greatest blessing.[8]

A Self-Revealing Process

We started part 4 with the notion that to find a belief in God that is meaningful, we must create our own concept of God from our inherent values and what inspires us. By looking actively for that God ideal in nature and in our self, we cultivate a warmth of heart toward our concept. Attention to the presence of our God ideal around us, as it intensifies, opens our heart. When that presence resonates with some aspect of our true inner nature, the magic of love awakens. Then we are able to go beyond mental musings and questions about whether God exists. Having deliberately chosen to create our own concept of God, we are awakening something in ourselves that remains dormant as long as the reach of our inquiry only goes as far as curiosity. We have a capacity to love. When we engage deep feelings of longing that have always smoldered beneath the surface, we awaken that capacity. An

---

7. Al-Hallaj, *Kitab al-Tawasin*, in *The Mystics of Islam* by Reynold A Nicholson, (London: Routledge, Kegan Paul, 1914), 151.
8. Hazrat Inayat Khan, *Gayan, Vadan, Nirtan*, 60.

open heart draws to us a state of realization that is not available to the mind. There is a knowledge that is self-revealing, kindled by a loving heart and heightened attention to what we truly care about, the ideals we love.

Hazrat Inayat Khan puts it poetically:

O Thou, the seed of my life's plant,
Thou wert hidden so long in my budlike soul;
but now Thou hast come out, O my life's fruit,
after the blossoming of my heart.[9]

It takes the blossoming of the heart for the seed nature of one's inner qualities to bring forth the fruit of God realization. By discovering the qualities dormant in one's inner self that are revealed in one's ideal, and by projecting that ideal on to the world outside us—every object in nature, animate and inanimate—the ideal comes alive as the Beloved. Then the God one has created becomes a reality. It is no longer a concept of God but a living presence. The Sufis would call it *Rabb*, the One to Whom I belong. When the heart is cultivated by the power of imagination focused on what one cares most about, the heart opens of its own accord and the love stream flowing through the heart transforms the God ideal into a living reality.

Sufi mystic Shahabuddin Suhrawardi called this kind of knowledge presential knowledge. It is a knowledge that comes through presence rather than through cogitation. Although it is self-revealing, it only reveals itself when the heart is kindled. It is not a knowledge composed of ideas but a knowing from direct experience. Ken Wilber calls it tasting. When we experience something directly through our senses, our experience is not a collection of ideas. Trying to describe it, we break it down into ideas. But the sensation itself is something whole, something we can't convey in words or

9. Ibid., 62.

ideas. Someone else's description of what it is like to taste an apple can't compare with our actual experience. In the same way, God realization can't be reduced to ideas or a description. It is a direct, ineffable experience, indescribable in words while also unlike any mundane experience. Yet, it is a real experience, not the result of imagination. To try to describe it would be profane because it inspires awe.

Realization has two meanings. It means knowledge that comes into awareness, like having an "aha" moment. It also means making something real or tangible. A striking edifice is the realization of an architect's plan. God realization is a transformative awareness of God as a reality as well as the realization or fulfillment of something in oneself. Something hidden has been made tangible. The seed in myself has brought forth fruit.

Seeking after God has brought about something perhaps unexpected. God has become a reality, something sensed directly, something that fulfills love's longing. At the same time, a maturing of self has happened. It is not just the feeling that I am one with everything, not just the loss of separation. It is as though what has been taken as the norm for human maturity is actually a raw and early stage of maturity. With God realization comes the full maturity of the human plant. It is the blossoming of the heart in the fullness of love that is possible when the object of love is the perfection of the Beloved. As long as the undercurrent of human longing is unsatisfied, full maturity is out of reach. The destiny of the human being is to be found in realizing the love capacity of the human heart.

Self-Realization

Are we not here in this world to be all that we can be, to play our particular role in revealing some aspect of the Hidden Treasure? Then we would want to follow the path of self-realization. However, Hazrat Inayat Khan writes, "It is not by self-realization that man realizes God; it is by God-realization that man realizes self."[10] What is the path of self-realization that one might pursue to try to realize God? Is it a development of the power of the self to achieve, to become knowledgeable, to behave ethically? Such a path may produce an admirable human with impressive accomplishments. However, it can also wall off God realization through pride in one's individuality. As Jesus said, "And again I say to you, it is easier for a camel to go through the eye of a needle than for a rich man to enter the kingdom of God" (Matthew 19:24). The richness of one's self-concept is the principal obstacle for realizing God. The path of the Sufi is called *fana'*, annihilation of the false self in the real. Of course, one starts on this path only after developing a healthy ego. Is there a conflict in this process? How can one realize self and be all that one is meant to be while emptying and turning away from self?

At the beginning of part 4, I quoted Hazrat Inayat Khan as saying, "God is the stepping-stone to the realization of self." Now we can understand that the God one makes from one's inherent ideal is necessary in this process. The God ideal is necessary for the alchemy of the heart and the magic of love to bring forth Self-realization. This kind of realization is not earmarked by impressive accomplishments in the world. Its sign is not what makes one exceptional. Its sign is the way it unites one with others. Its sign is through harmony, love, and unity. It can be read in the eyes when the quality of the

10. Ibid., 18.

heart shows through. The true maturity of the human being is found in the heart, not in the mind.

We started this journey considering the idea of the atheists that science has replaced the need for an all-powerful personal God to explain the frightening phenomena of the world. Nowadays, we no longer feel a need to appease God to ward off flood and famine. Darwin has explained the dazzling designs of nature as gradual adaptations to a changeable environment, eliminating the need for a providential Creator. Atheists would have rationality replace faith which they hold to be naive. Turning to God in prayer is seen to be wishful thinking. Better to take up one's responsibility with courage and make the best of one's life.

Now we have arrived at a markedly different idea. God is not something that can be investigated scientifically as stated in the God hypothesis or arrived at philosophically through reason and logic. God is a stepping-stone for our own fulfillment, for stimulating and cultivating a Hidden Treasure buried in each heart. Creating our own God ideal based on what is inherent in our psyche is a catalyst for a process that, once set in motion, leads to realization of the true self and ultimately to Self-realization.

God and Religion

Each of us is unique. Were we to create our own God ideal, it too, would be unique. Once asked, "How many beliefs about God are there in the world?" Indian Vedanta master Swami Vivekananda answered, "as many as there are people." If we have a belief in God and are religious, we are likely to feel we share our belief with others of our religion and perhaps question the beliefs of other religions. What if everyone's belief were based on their inherent values? Religion would come from within rather than being the property of a church or scripture. We would belong to the religion of the heart, an essence of religion that can be found in all outward religions. Sufi mystic Ibn 'Arabi felt this religion of the heart was his religion.

> O Marvel, a garden among the flames!
> My heart can take on any form: a meadow for ga-
>   zelles, a cloister for monks,
> For the idols, sacred ground, Kaba for the circling
>   pilgrim, the tables of the Torah, the scrolls of the
>   Qur'an.
> I profess the religion of love; wherever its caravan
>   turns along the way, that is the belief, the faith I
>   keep.[11]

The religion of love is found at the root of each of the world's major religions.

The Abrahamic religions of Judaism, Christianity, and Islam have each taught their followers to praise and worship God, to trust in God as Judge and Sustainer, and to be humble and caring toward others and nature. These practices uplift one by holding a divine ideal before one's imagination and subdue the ego by urging it to think of others before oneself.

There is great variety in the practice of the Hindu religion. The avatars Rama, Krishna, and Shiva similarly stimulate and uplift the imagination by the projection of one's ideal. The ego is subdued by bowing before one's ideal as well as by the tradition of *vairagya* in which, once one has fulfilled one's duties to family, one can leave everyday life behind and dedicate oneself to spiritual matters.

Buddhism dispenses with the concept of God. One is instead inspired by the eightfold way, by aspiring to live up to

11. Ibn 'Arabi, *Tarjuman al-Ashwaq*, translation by Michael Sells in *Stations of Desire* (Jerusalem: Ibis Editions, 2000), 51.

one's ideals. Buddha taught that there is no individual self, the principle of *anatma*, and no individual soul. Living up to one's ideals is not for the ego or self. It is for the termination of suffering. When one lets go of the fears and worries of the ego and lets the sense of self become fluid and free, one begins to develop serenity.

What Is God?

Is God merely a temporary device by which we enhance our imagination to achieve self-realization? The ego is a devious deceiver. If self-realization were a goal to reward the ego, then the process I have described would be suspect. Mystics have made it clear that the ego stands in the way of realization. It is our selfishness that keeps our heart closed. Remember that infatuation softens the ego of the youth, causing the youth to think of the welfare of the beloved before self. This process is intensified and expanded in the mystical quest. There is a Jewish belief that one cannot face God and continue to live. The mystical meaning of this belief is that one must die to the ego before one can encounter the Beloved. The Sufi mystic Muinuddin Chishti says,

> The one who knows becomes perfect only when
> all else is removed from in-between him and the
> Friend.
> Either he remains or the Friend.[12]

Thus, there is nothing for the ego to gain in achieving God realization, and God realization leads to Self-realization.

---

12. Muinuddin Chishti, "Living from the Heart: Sayings of Hazrat Khwaja Mu'inuddin Hassan Chishti," Wahiduddin's Web, https://wahiduddin.net/sufi/muinuddin_sayings.htm.

What then is this God ideal one creates for oneself? It is an imagination, but it is also a reflection of something real within oneself. It is impossible to see one's eyes without a mirror. Similarly, one cannot see one's soul without finding it in a reflection. Through imagination, one reflects back to oneself something that is real within oneself. The soul is said to be an action of God or a ray of the primal sun. The God ideal one creates by reflecting the nature of one's inner ideal is then a limited image of something real but invisible. By establishing a relationship with it, by opening one's heart to it, it becomes a presence, a direct experience rather than a concept. Like tasting an apple. Eventually the presence becomes more real than one's self-image, which is nothing more than a concept. The God ideal as a limited reflection then falls away and is replaced by an undeniable reality. Hazrat Inayat Khan says, "Shatter your ideals upon the rock of Truth."[13]

What is it that becomes real? Is it a mirage, a hallucination? Rather, it is a truth that has always been there inside. The practitioners of Dzogchen say one can't become spiritual because one has always been spirit. The truth of one's being is universal Spirit. Seeing its reflection in the God ideal awakens one to its reality, the only Reality. One could say that God realization, discovering the reality of the One Being, is the same as Self-realization, discovering the reality of One Self.

Hazrat Inayat Khan records the experience of awakening to the Truth:

> I first believed without any hesitation in the existence of the soul, and then I wondered about the secret of its nature. I persevered and strove in search of the soul, and found at last that I myself was the cover over my soul. I realized that that in me which believed and that

13. Hazrat Inayat Khan, *Gayan, Vadan, Nirtan*, 115.

in me which wondered, that which persevered in me, and that which found, and that which was found at last, was no other than my soul. I thanked the darkness that had brought me to the light, and I valued the veil which prepared for me the vision in which I saw myself reflected, the vision produced in the mirror of my soul. Since then I have seen all souls as my soul, and realized my soul as the soul of all. And what bewilderment it was when I realized that I alone was, if there were anyone; that I am whatever and whoever exists; and that I shall be whoever there will be in the future. And there was no end to my happiness and joy.

Verily, I am the seed and I am the root and I am the fruit of this tree of life.[14]

14. Hazrat Inayat Khan, "The Phenomenon of the Soul," in *Spiritual Liberty*, vol. V, *The Sufi Message of Hazrat Inayat Khan* (London: Barrie and Rockliff, 1962), 137.

Inayatiyya

A Sufi Path of Spiritual Liberty

Sulūk Press is an independent publisher dedicated to issuing works of spirituality and cultural moment, with a focus on Sufism, in particular, the works of Hazrat Inayat Khan and his successors. To learn more about Inayatiyya Sufism, please visit **inayatiyya.org**.

www.ingramcontent.com/pod-product-compliance
Lightning Source LLC
Jackson TN
JSHW021354171224
75420JS00007B/137